RETRO RIDE

About the Author

A hard-core wheelman, Tony Swan has been involved with automobiles for over 30 years. He has held editorial positions with *Cycle World*, *Sports Car Graphic*, *Motor Trend*, and *Popular Mechanics* and won several journalism awards for his auto review columns. Currently serving as Executive Editor of *Car and Driver* magazine, Swan is also a veteran sports car racer.

The publisher would like to extend a special thanks to Richard and Linda Rosemus who provided access to their vast magazine advertising collection. Without their generous help this book would not have been possible. Thank you is also extended to Lisa Perry, Lori Cunningham, Felicia Caravone, and Amy Flax for their organizational assistance.

Design *Evan Holt, Collectors Press, Inc.*
Editor *Lisa Perry*

For a Free Catalog write to:

COLLECTORS PRESS, INC.

P.O. Box 230986
Portland, OR 97281
Toll free 1 800 423 1848
www.collectorspress.com

Printed in Hong Kong

First American Edition

987654321

Library of Congress Cataloging-in-Publication Data

Swan, Tony, 1940-
    Retro ride : advertising art of the American automobile / by Tony
Swan.
       p. cm.
    ISBN 1-888054-62-X (alk. paper)
    1. Advertising—Automobiles—United States—History. 2.
Automobiles—United States—History.   I. Title.
    HF6161.A9 S93 2002
    659.1'96292'0973—dc21
                                                    2001006500

PORTLAND, OREGON

RETRO RIDE

ADVERTISING ART OF THE
AMERICAN AUTOMOBILE

It's the "HIS" and "HER" car

USA 1958

Big · Bold · Buoyant

Flight Pitch Dynaflow standard on LIMITED and ROADMASTER 75, optional at extra cost on other Series. Air-Poise Suspension optional at extra cost on all Series.

The '49 Ford has been awarded the Fashion Academy Gold Medal as the 'Fashion Car of the Year'

It's a Dream Wagon...this '49 FORD
with its (heart) of steel and the new FORD "FEEL"!

It's steel, steel, steel.

Yes, it's all steel—even under that gleaming molded plywood paneling. It's Ford's famous all-steel "Lifeguard" body, welded into a rigid unit for even greater strength and safety. Truly a heart of steel, wrapped in luxury!

It's sealed against dust.

The convenient easy-opening tailgate—as well as the doors—is completely weather-sealed to guard against annoying dust and water leaks. Here's a feature you'll certainly appreciate, especially when you're touring.

Feel that safety!

This new Ford "Dream Wagon" has two wide doors instead of four narrow doors, a blessing to parents of small children. There's more visibility all around, and the safer, surer stopping of King-Size brakes that are 35% easier acting.

And feel that comfort!

There's plenty of room for eight big people, plus a ride that's in a class by itself—thanks to new "Hydra-Coil" front springs and new "Para-Flex" rear springs that smooth out the roughest roads!

Feel that power!

You'll love this great car's performance . . . it's powered with the famous 100 h.p. Ford V-8, the same type of engine used in America's costliest cars. Why not see the new Ford Station Wagon today? Take the wheel—try the new Ford "Feel"!

"Take the Wheel try the new Ford Feel"

There's a *New* Ford in your future

White side wall tires, optional at extra cost.

All eyes are on the "Rocket"! All eyes are on the most exciting motor car

on the highway! It's Oldsmobile's sensational "88"—lowest-priced car with the "Rocket"

Engine and Oldsmobile Hydra-Matic*. Try that "Rocket Ride" yourself!

OLDSMOBILE

"88"

THE "ROCK

HYDRA-MAT

CAR!

*dra-Matic Drive optional at
a cost on all Oldsmobile models.

US 6

A General Motors V

INTRODUCTION

In the beginning, there was the automobile, an amalgam of 19th century technologies that seemed an unlikely agent of massive social change. Evolving during an extraordinary period of invention that also saw the advent of the electric light, the phonograph, wireless telegraphy, the telephone, and powered flight, the early automobile was primitive, quirky, temperamental, and lacked the tried-and-true reliability of horse-drawn conveyances. On the other hand, there were also some very appealing traits. For example, although the machinery that propelled these early cars was fragile, when something ceased to function, an automobile could be repaired, rather than shot, or converted to glue, the usual fate of broken-down horses. And, not to put too fine a point on it, in the realm of emissions, automobiles were infinitely more appealing than quadrupeds. We didn't know about oxides of nitrogen and carbon monoxide in those days. We did, however, have a well developed sense of the byproducts of equine internal combustion. More important, though it was crude, the automobile offered vast potential for development. A horse, for its part, was a horse.

While its initial prospects may have seemed tenuous in their day -- beyond the fragility of the machine itself, there was almost no national highway system (200 miles of paved in 1900, almost all of it urban), and no supporting infrastructure (service stations were yet to be invented) -- the horseless carriage obviously survived its infancy. Although dozens of would-be carmakers came and went, some lasting only a matter of months, the automobile advanced from a novelty to something much more significant.

In fact, it's not an exaggeration to say that no invention has had as much impact on everyday life as the automobile. Although debate will probably never end as to whether this impact is good or bad, it's inarguably clear that the automobile has left an indelible imprint on society -- particularly American society. For example, the automobile -- in particular, the Model T Ford automobile -- was instrumental in changing America from a largely rural nation to an urban one. It was also the critical element in the rise of the suburbs.

Well, that was then, this is now, and automobiles, in all their bewildering 21st century variety -- cars, trucks, minivans, sport-utilities -- are as indispensable to most of us as clothing, food, and breathing, and it's all but impossible to imagine a time when this wasn't so. In fact, it became hard to remember that automobiles hadn't always been part of daily life not long after World War I. When America roared into the Twenties, a mere two-plus decades into the 20th century, the automobile was well on its way to becoming the dominant transportation device in this country.

What had happened to stimulate such dramatic change in such a short span of time? For one thing, automobiles became available to ordinary people, rather than the wealthy few. We can thank Henry Ford for that. The crude but rugged Model T Ford, which became more and more affordable throughout a production run spanning almost two decades, thanks to modern moving assembly line techniques and consequent economies of scale, put motoring within range of millions of people in America and the world at large. At one point, half the cars on the planet were Model Ts, and when production finally ended in 1927, the tally stood at over 15 million -- a production record that stood for decades.

But the evolution of practical automobiles was only part of the story. In order to take advantage of mass production, there had to be mass markets. Which meant communicating with those potential markets. Which meant advertising.

Henry Ford's vision for the Model T was compelling -- the illusion of virtually unlimited personal mobility for everyone. But it took more than the sight of a Tin Lizzie to fire the imaginations of potential customers. And in the years following World War I, magazine advertising began to whet American automotive appetites with increasing skill, creating needs, real or imagined, as well as conveying hard product information. Not to mention the creation and amplification of image, the idea that your automobile helped to define who you were, or at least how you wished to be perceived.

As the decades rolled by, automobiles became more technically sophisticated, as well as more diverse, and automobile advertising kept pace, quickly shifting gears from hardware descriptions to flights of fancy designed to tantalize the well-heeled, sophisticated nomad dwelling in every man. As often as not, the aim was seduction, rather than a straight sales pitch, supported by striking four-color illustrations. Perhaps the most memorable example of this approach was the famous ad for the 1923 Jordan Playboy that opened with a fanciful dateline: "Somewhere west of Laramie." Ned Jordan's immortal ad copy had nothing to with crankshafts, horsepower, or carburetion and everything to do with romantic escapism, lending definition to the dream that made the automobile so appealing to begin with. "Somewhere west of Laramie there's a broncho-busting, steer-roping girl who knows what I'm talking about. "She can tell what a sassy pony, that's a cross between greased lightning and the place where it hits, can do with eleven hundred pounds of steel and action when he's going high, wide and handsome. The truth is, the Playboy was built for her. Built for the lass whose face is brown with the sun when the day is done of revel and romp and race.

"She loves the cross of the wild and the tame.

"There's a savor of links about that car-of laughter and lilt and light -- a hint of old lovers -- and saddle and quirt. It's a brawny thing -- yet a graceful thing for the sweep o' the avenue.

"Step into the Playboy when the hour grows dull with things gone dead and stale.

"Then start for the land of real living, with the spirit of the lass who rides, lean and rangy, into the red horizon of a Wyoming twilight."

Though Jordan's uninhibited hyperbole helped to set the stage for countless blood-red sunsets and moon-drenched beaches in succeeding generations of advertising copy writers, the transition from tech-oriented feature-benefit text was neither instantaneous nor universal. We still see advertisements booming the capabilities and benefits of the latest technological innovations -- braking by wire, for example, or electronic stability enhancements, or fuel cells -- and we always will.

And in this sense -- technical development -- print advertising provides an interesting record of the mechanical evolution of the automobile. Interesting, as distinct from objective. These were the days before advertisers had the Federal Trade Commission looking over their shoulders to make sure their assertions were based on verifiable facts. Still, even though every car seemed to represent the absolute latest in technical advancement, to judge by the claims, a cross section of ads over the years tracks developments quite accurately. An irrefutably better idea -- hydraulic brakes, overhead valves, automatic transmissions -- shows up in one manufacturer's ad, and within a couple of years has spread across the entire industry. Similarly, there are consistent themes -- power, comfort, style, image, and safety -- that carry through from one decade to the next.

In contrast, even though the style of the language evolves, thus reflecting contemporary usage, and the fashions of the models reflect their times, there is an intriguing uniformity to the presentations suggesting an America that has been uniquely free of hard times. Aside from the World War II years, the collected reflections assembled here, including samples from the depths of the Great Depression, provide a picture of a society that's prosperous, well-ordered, and happy.

This book traces the simultaneous evolution of the automobile and the marketing messages that helped to provide it with an increasingly diverse persona across five decades -- the Roaring Twenties through the Go-Go Sixties. The era was the heyday of American print advertising. During this period magazines had no rival as a medium for bright, imaginative, and compelling presentation of automobiles, which had risen from almost total obscurity to the biggest single advertising category. Radio was a major player, too, but not for products like automobiles. And it took TV some two decades to effectively exploit its dynamic advantages.

The images in this anthology reflect not only the products, but the times in which they flourished. It's a unique look at an America that was. And it's a ride well worth the taking.

Tony Swan

CHEV

for Everybod

A SIX IN THE PRICE

OLET

Everywhere

RANGE OF THE FOUR

A Principle Consistently Adhered To

The avowed purpose behind the building of the Lincoln is to make this car beyond question the finest that can be built.

Precision—workmanship and a keen sense of responsibility on the part of the capable Lincoln organization has accomplished the fulfillment of this pledge.

It is with pride, therefore, that the builders of the Lincoln have witnessed the growing admiration for the beauty, performance and lasting service of this car. They find reward for their efforts in the steadily increasing conviction on the part of the public—that here, truly, is the supreme automotive achievement, backed by an organization pledged to keep it supreme.

LINCOLN MOTOR COMPANY
Division of Ford Motor Company, Detroit, Michigan

The Phaeton

LINCOLN

1923 LINCOLN THE PHAETON

Her habit of measuring time in terms of dollars gives the woman in business keen insight into the true value of a Ford closed car for her personal use.

This car enables her to conserve minutes, to expedite her affairs, to widen the scope of her activities. Its low first cost, long life and inexpensive operation and upkeep convince her that it is a sound investment value.

And it is such a pleasant car to drive that it transforms the business call which might be an interruption into an enjoyable episode of her busy day.

CLOSED CARS

1924 FORD
CLOSED CARS

1924 FORD CLOSED CARS

1925 Cadillac

LINCOLN

Even a superficial acquaintance with the Lincoln is sufficient to create a dominant impression of distinction and individuality.

LINCOLN MOTOR COMPANY
Division of
FORD MOTOR COMPANY

1924 Lincoln

PRECISION
Everyone admires the dignity of the Lincoln's outward beauty, but only those of advanced technical understanding fully appreciate the marvel of its mechanical perfection

LINCOLN MOTOR COMPANY
Division of
Ford Motor Company

LINCOLN

THE LINCOLN HAS WON
NATION-WIDE ACCEPTANCE

IN ALL parts of the country, the Lincoln is known as a fast, easy-riding, smooth-running, and long-lived car. Its beauty is admired, its abilities respected. Through brilliant qualities of performance and soundness of construction, it has definitely established itself in the good opinion of the nation as a car of outstanding and enduring worth.

See any Lincoln Dealer

LINCOLN MOTOR COMPANY
DIVISION OF FORD MOTOR CO., DETROIT, MICH.

The Phaeton

LINCOLN

1924 Lincolns

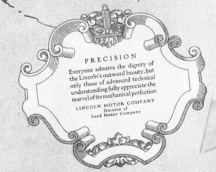

The Human Desire to Own the Best Suggests *the* Cadillac

Own the Car You Long Have Wanted

Value more remarkable than that of this fine Cadillac Coach is simply not to be had in the motor car market.

For Cadillac has built—not merely a closed car at open car price—but a closed car in which outstanding value, quality and beauty go hand in hand.

Those who have viewed the Coach, who have observed the elegance and

comfort of its large five-passenger body and experienced the powerful, vibrationless performance of the V-63 eight-cylinder chassis, tell us that the car confers new meaning upon Coach design.

And so, in steadily increasing numbers, discriminating purchasers are acquiring this fine Cadillac Coach, fulfilling their desire to own the best.

$3185
f. o. b. Detroit

CADILLAC MOTOR CAR COMPANY, DETROIT, MICHIGAN
Division of General Motors Corporation

CADILLAC COACH
STANDARD OF THE WORLD

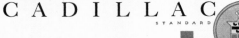
1925 Cadillac Coach

1925 Ford

LINCOLN

1925 Lincolns

LINCOLN

Today's Lincolns reflect the art of the designer who has had untrammeled opportunity to carry out his best ideas.

LINCOLN MOTOR COMPANY
Division of
Ford Motor Company

LINCOLN

The remarkable precision methods now employed in producing the superb 60° V-Type Lincoln motor are attracting wide comment throughout the motoring world.

LINCOLN MOTOR COMPANY
Division of
Ford Motor Company

1925 LINCOLN 60 DEGREE V-TYPE

"The supreme combination of all that is fine in motor cars."

Quality. True quality in man or motor car is a subtle blending, a well balanced combination, of many fine traits.

THE RESTFUL CAR

Packard quality, like that which distinguished the gentry of our ancestral tradition, is bred in the bone. It is the result of more than a quarter century of evolution from that first Packard which a genius of great means built to surpass any car then produced.

So the Packard comes of a distinguished family of fine cars—long supreme in every characteristic which quality demands—long accepted into intimate association with the great.

And the latest scion of this line—the improved Packard of today—is earning by conquest the right to its title "The Greatest Car in the World." Appreciation of its quality—its superiority in every point of comparison—can come only with ownership. The improved Packard has no peers.

PACKARD

Ask the man who owns one

1925 PACKARD

LINCOLN

The low, trim Sport Phaeton, designed by Brunn, includes among its smart touches a tan top with mahogany bows. Wire wheels carried forward. Tonneau cowl and windshield available if desired.

LINCOLN MOTOR COMPANY
Division of
Ford Motor Company

1926 LINCOLN PHAETON

LINCOLN

For the growing number of people who prefer an open car for personal use, there is none so satisfying nor of more unmistakable style than the powerful Lincoln Sport Roadster with body by Locke.

LINCOLN MOTOR COMPANY
Division of
Ford Motor Company

1926 LINCOLN SPORT ROADSTER

1926 LINCOLN CABRIOLET

LINCOLN

In the two-passenger Coupe, Judkins has admirably interpreted the fleetness and power of the Lincoln in the sweep and symmetry of body lines.

LINCOLN MOTOR COMPANY
Division of
Ford Motor Company

1926 LINCOLN TWO-PASSENGER COUPE

LINCOLN

For formal use there is no more distinguished equipage than the Lincoln Cabriolet, with collapsible rear quarter, designed and built by Brunn.

LINCOLN MOTOR COMPANY
Division of
Ford Motor Company

Make This Christmas last for thousands of miles . . . .

A **B**UICK *for* **C**hristmas

1927 BUICK

1927 BUICK

"The supreme combination of all that is fine in motor cars."

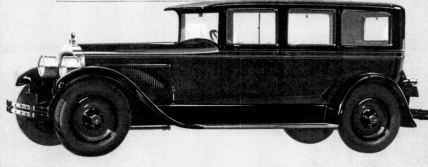

1926 PACKARD

PRIDE of ownership is the result of quality. Every Buick owner is proud of the car he drives—proud of its smart beauty, proud of its sterling dependability, and especially, proud of its powerful engine, *vibrationless beyond belief.*

BUICK

1927 BUICK

1927 Buicks

The Unexpected - is the *Expected thing* in Buick

One outstanding reason for the unqualified enthusiasm of Buick owners for their cars, is Buick's ability to meet the *unexpected* in daily driving.

The instant response of the powerful Buick *Valve-in-Head* Engine in time of need; the quick, positive action of Buick's *mechanical* Four-Wheel Brakes in an emergency; Buick's endurance under conditions which would stop an ordinary car—these lead Buick owners to expect performance from Buick which other cars would never be asked to give.

Buy a Buick for sterling performance—for economy, dependability, luxury, beauty and unmatched value.

BUICK MOTOR COMPANY, FLINT, MICH.
Division of General Motors Corporation
Canadian Factories: McLAUGHLIN-BUICK, Oshawa, Ontario.

Beauty

Beauty that surpasses all tradition

Buick, today, is an expression of exquisite beauty—surpassing in its artistry all other motor car design.

Buick

WHEN BETTER AUTOMOBILES ARE BUILT - BUICK WILL BUILD THEM

1927 Buick

THE way the Chrysler Imperial "80" delivers, at long continued high speeds, its 92 horsepower in a quiet, soft, smooth steadiness hitherto unknown, has evoked an enthusiasm that has contributed not a little to the phenomenal advance of Chrysler from twenty-seventh to fourth place—in three years.

The superlative ease of the Imperial "80"— the way its power *flows* in a twinkling from a snail's pace to sixty, seventy, eighty or more miles per hour—the way it flashes in and out of traffic, nimbly outdistancing the fastest and finest—these are the symbols of the supreme motoring luxury into which Chrysler has translated 92 horsepower in the Imperial "80".

CHRYSLER SALES CORPORATION, DETROIT, MICHIGAN
CHRYSLER CORPORATION OF CANADA, LIMITED, WINDSOR, ONTARIO

CHRYSLER IMPERIAL "80"

1927 Chrysler Imperial "80"

1927 Essex Super-Six

Riding is like *flying*

You can never forget this thrilling difference from all other transportation!

Smooth indifference to road conditions . . . Silky smoothness in all performance . . . Riding in the Essex Super-Six is actually like flying.

The dramatic appeal of a single ride is the basis of the greatest sales in our history.

This amazing Super-Six performance and quality is economical to buy and own. It is the outstanding triumph of engineering—for long wear, accessibility and lowest operation and maintenance costs.

ESSEX
Super-Six

The 2-Passenger
Speedabout
$700

4-pass. Speedster . . . $785
Coupe 735
Coach 735
Sedan 795

1927 Lincoln Sport Touring

The Lincoln on the Boulevards of the World
Washington Boulevard, Detroit

Sport Touring

Body by Fisher

1928 Buick

MOTORISTS everywhere acknowledge the New Cadillac for its modern charm, its size, its luxury. But those who drive it will be so enthralled by its amazing resources

of eager power that, to them, the New Cadillac will ever mean power—power in abundance that does the exceptional with matter-of-fact ease and brilliant finality.

More than 50 exclusive body styles by Fisher and Fisher-Fleetwood

CADILLAC
A Notable Product of General Motors

1928 Cadillac

The Bentley Car

"The supreme combination of all that is fine in motor cars."

1927 Packard

JUST as Cadillac beauty created a vogue in motor car style, so has Cadillac's incomparable performance re-created a vogue for driving. There is an irresistible desire to take the wheel of the Cadillac and enjoy what none but a Cadillac-built car, with its 90-degree, V-type, 8-cylinder engine, can give—performance seemingly unlimited in range and variety, so unlabored, so easily controlled, so zestful yet restful, that once again Cadillac has given the idea of luxury in motoring a new meaning.

More than 50 exclusive body styles by Fisher and Fisher-Fleetwood

CADILLAC

A NOTABLE PRODUCT OF GENERAL MOTORS

1928 CADILLAC

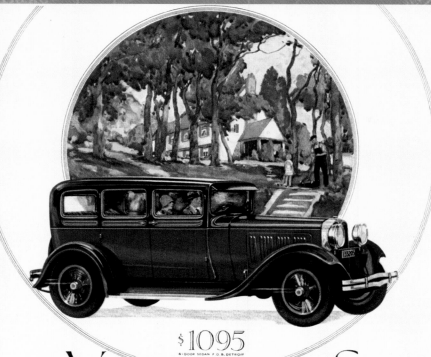

$1095
4-DOOR SEDAN F.O.B. DETROIT

The VICTORY SIX

The Sport Sedan

Lines that critical eyes approve

1928 Dodge The Victory Six Sport Sedan

1928 Dodge New Four

ESSEX SUPER SIX

World's Greatest Value

as all the World Knows

The Essex Super-Six is outselling, and all this year has outsold, every other "Six" by such margins that comparison is only a gesture.

Not only in Detroit, where automobile values are better understood than anywhere in the world, but in New England and the South; in the West, the Orient and the Antipodes its popular prefer-ence is instant, sustained and eagerly increasing.

For it needs no expert to see—what every expert knows—that such an array of values was never before presented within hundreds of dollars of the price.

To know the overpowering conviction of great-est value held by Essex owners is merely to see Essex beauty, to examine Essex quality, to sit inside and feel Essex comfort — to ride and know Essex performance.

The Essex 4-Door Sedan

1928 Essex Super Six Four Door Sedan

WORLD'S GREATEST VALUE

Fine Car Transportation

At Lowest Cost per Mile

FOUR-DOOR SEDAN, $795 f. o. b. Detroit

The New ESSEX Super-Six

In the way women by thousands are turning to Essex is a story of the great and dynamic "man's Super-Six" made beautiful for women—roomy and comfortable for all the family.

You sit upon high-back, form-fitting seats upholstered in material that tells its quality to sight and to the touch. The winged radiator figure leads the eye out over a shin-ing rhythm of cowl, hood, polished saddle type lamps and graceful arching fenders to the smoothly flying highroad.

You have before you every control in their most natural and handy place. And all about you, the paneling, the weather-stripped doors, the silenced body construction, the floor-matting and the hardware in graceful silvery patterns speak quietly and certainly of quality.

In these and such things as the slender black rubber, steel-core, finger-scalloped steering wheel; the worm and tooth disc steering mechanism and the vertical radiator shutters, Essex visibly duplicates costly car practice, as it does also in the hidden things you never see.

HUDSON MOTOR CAR COMPANY DETROIT, MICHIGAN

1928 Essex Super Six Four Door Sedan

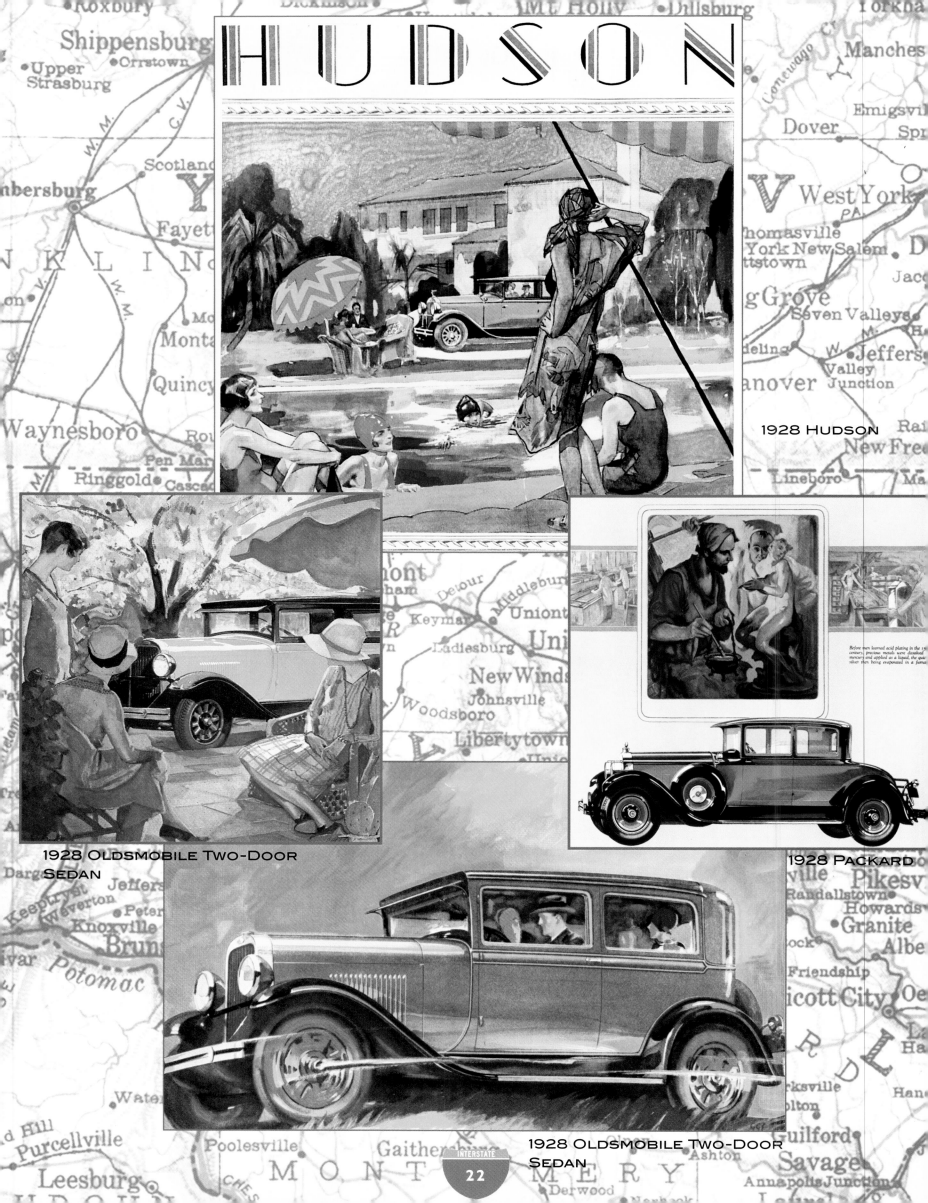

HUDSON

1928 Hudson

1928 Oldsmobile Two-Door
Sedan

1928 Packard

1928 Oldsmobile Two-Door
Sedan

22

A Marvelous Improvement in *Cold Weather Performance*

Body by Fisher

-*a Successful Six* now winning Even Greater Success

1928 PONTIAC SIX

The 2-Door Sedan, $745

A new order of performance in General Motors' *lowest priced six*

Remember when Pontiac Six was introduced some thirty months ago, how it scored a record-breaking success? How it established a new order of performance among low-priced sixes by combining smoothness, snap and Fisher body luxury with unfaltering endurance? . . . No less impressively does today's Pontiac Six tower above the field —because in performance, as in all other phases, it represents a policy of continuous advancement! . . . In view of such exclusive engineering developments as the cross-flow radiator and the G-M-R cylinder head—such size as is typified by a 186-cubic inch engine —such unrivaled length of life as Pontiac owners enjoy . . . small wonder that everyone acclaims the new order of performance revealed by General Motors' lowest-priced six.

Pontiac Six, $745 to $875. All prices at factory.

OAKLAND MOTOR CAR CO., PONTIAC, MICHIGAN

PONTIAC SIX

-*a Successful Six* now winning Even Greater Success

1928 PONTIAC SIX TWO-DOOR SEDAN

1929 BUICK

1929 BUICK

1929 BUICK MODEL 47
FOUR-DOOR SEDAN

1929 CHEVROLET

LA SALLE

1929 CADILLAC LA SALLE

The Literary Digest for March 9, 1929

$695 at factory and up

LLENGER

1929 ESSEX

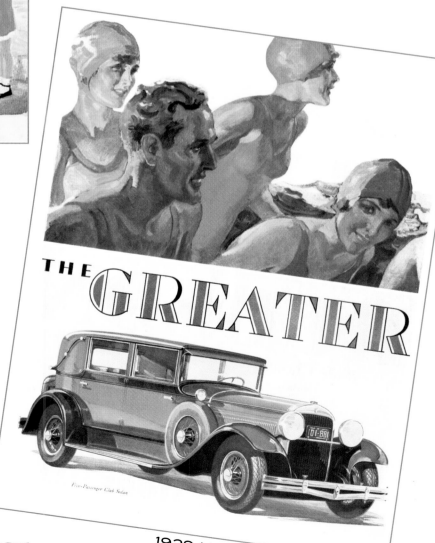

THE GREATER

1929 HUDSON CLUB SEDAN

HUDSON

1929 Hudson Landau Sedan

1929 Hupmobile

Hudson 127-inch
Landau Sedan

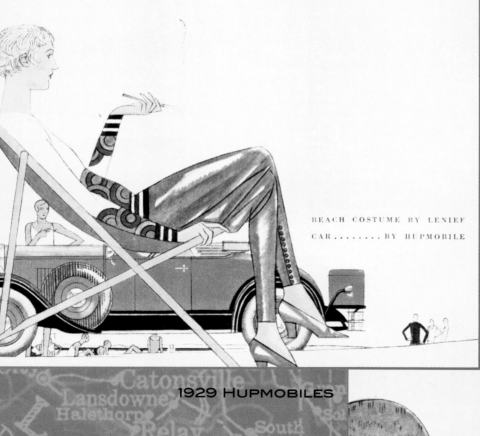

BEACH COSTUME BY LENIEF
CAR........BY HUPMOBILE

1929 Hupmobiles

US
26

1929 Pontiac Big Six

1929 Packard

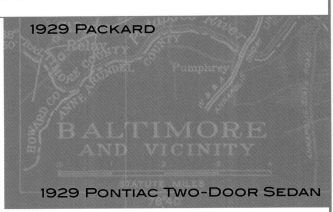

1929 Pontiac Two-Door Sedan

1930 Buick Straight Eight

RECEPTION TO THE
DIPLOMATIC CORPS
AT THE WHITE HOUSE

IN the press of fine cars at diplomatic and state functions in the nation's capital, motor cars by Studebaker are rightfully high in favor. ••• These great new Studebaker eights and sixes hold every official stock car record for speed and endurance. Their fleetness and untiring endurance are splendidly interpreted in low-swung lines, fluent curves and delightfully new color schemes. ••• There is a revelation awaiting you in your first scrutiny of what Studebaker's unique One-Profit manufacture has wrought. ••• The car illustrated is the President Straight Eight Brougham for five.

Studebaker
BUILDER OF CHAMPIONS

1929 Studebaker President Straight Eight Brougham

1929 Viking 90 Degree V-Eight

for Economical Transportation

CHEVROLET

IT'S WISE TO CHOOSE A SIX

The Chevrolet 6-cylinder coach

1930 CHEVROLET SIX COACH
AND SIX CLUB SEDANS

for Economical Transportation
CHEVROLET
IT'S WISE TO CHOOSE A SIX

HOMETOWN 100 MILES

Buying 5 gallons of gasoline to cover a distance of 100 miles, is a common experience among owners of the Chevrolet Six. Illustrated is the Chevrolet Coach, $565 at the factory.

Chevrolet's liberal service policy protects every Chevrolet owner

There is comfort and satisfaction in knowing—when you invest in a Chevrolet Six—that a liberal service policy will protect you wherever you care to drive. Under the terms of the Chevrolet Owner's Service Policy, any one of Chevrolet's 10,000 dealers anywhere in the United States or Canada will make regular free inspections every thousand miles through-

out the life of the car. Any Chevrolet dealer will make replacements with no charge for parts or labor, as specified in the new Chevrolet Owner's Service Policy! Think how much more satisfying it is to own a car with this protection —how much more economical! Think how dependable a car must be to warrant such a liberal service policy!

CHEVROLET SIX

FEATURES: 50-horsepower six-cylinder motor . . . de luxe wire wheels at no extra cost . . . a variety of attractive colors . . . modern, long, semi-elliptic springs . . . fully enclosed four-wheel brakes Fisher hardwood-and-steel bodies . . . safety gasoline tank in the rear . . . and, for your protection, a new and liberal Chevrolet service policy.

Chevrolet Motor Company, Detroit, Michigan, Division of General Motors Corporation

for Economical Transportation
CHEVROLET
IT'S WISE TO

The Chevrolet Club Sedan with Body by Fisher is an unusual example of smart closed car styling. Five wire wheels standard equipment. $665, f.o.b. factory, Flint

...der satisfaction without cost for gas, oil or upkeep

Every day the swing to the Six in the low-price field grows steadily bigger and more impressive. For people everywhere are learning that the new Chevrolet not only gives all the advantages of six-cylinder smoothness, power, flexibility and comfort —but does so without added cost for operation or upkeep.

In a recent officially-observed economy run, a Chevrolet six-cylinder Coach won first place, averaging better than twenty miles to the gallon. No automobile surpasses Chevrolet in oil economy. No car offers owners the benefits of more efficient service than that available at more than 10,000 authorized Chevrolet service sta-

tions—where on many service and repair operations the flat-rate charges—including both parts and labor—are the lowest in the automotive industry.

And Chevrolet six-cylinder smoothness saves the entire car—engine, chassis and body—from the strain and wear of constant vibration. This, of course, lowers the cost of maintenance and assures a longer lasting, more satisfying automobile. As a result of these basic economy factors, the Chevrolet Six costs as little to own and operate as any car on the road today. And it can be bought on a small down payment and easy monthly terms!

CHEVROLET MOTOR COMPANY, DETROIT, MICH.
Division of General Motors Corporation

CHEVROLET SIX

Sport Roadster..$555   Club Sedan...$665
Coach.........$565   Sedan........$675   ROADSTER or PHAETON   Sedan Delivery
Coupe.........$565   Special Sedan..$725
Sport Coupe...$655   (6 wire wheels standard on Special Sedan)

$495

Announcing a new production...

2,000,000 Chevrolet Sixes now on the road

Since January, 1929, the Chevrolet Motor Company has produced and sold over 2,000,000 six-cylinder automobiles.

Such impressive public preference reveals the extent to which buyers of low-priced cars are insisting on the advantages of six-cylinder design. And it proves in no uncertain terms that it's wise to choose a Chevrolet Six!

These 2,000,000 buyers have chosen Chevrolet because it offers the smoothness, silence and flexibility of a modern six-cylinder engine—the comfort and road-

ability of a full-length chassis with up-to-date spring suspension—the style and distinction of bodies by Fisher—and the safety assured by hardwood-and-steel body construction combined with the gasoline tank at the rear of the...

Yet, despite these fine car advantages, the Chevrolet Six is unusually economical. Its gas, oil, tire and upkeep costs are unsurpassed. And any model may be bought for a small down payment and easy monthly terms!

CHEVROLET MOTOR COMPANY
Division of General Motors...

CHEVROLET

$495

Sport Roadster..$555   Club Sedan...$665   ROADSTER or PHAETON   Sedan Delivery
Coach.........$565   Sedan........$675   Light Delivery
Coupe.........$565   Special Sedan..$725   Chassis....
Sport Coupe...$655   (6 wire wheels standard on Special Sedan) Roadster Delivery (Pick-up box)

"Women must have influenced the design of that car. It is so smart and delightful to drive."

The NEW

ESSEX *Challenger*

US 30

1930 ESSEX

Beauty of line and mechanical excellence

1930 Ford Town Sedan

1930 Ford Three-Window Fordor Sedan

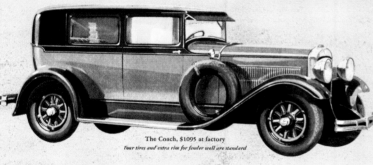

The Standard Sedan, $1175 at factory
Spare tire carried in right fender well, with luggage rack in rear

HUDSON

The Coupe, $1195 at factory
Four wheels and tire with extra rim are standard

1930 Hudson The Standard Sedan, The Coupe

1930 Hudson The Coach, The Town Sedan

1930 Hudson Great Eight

The Coach, $1095 at factory
Four tires and extra rim for fender well are standard

The Town Sedan, $1375 at factory
Five demountable wheels in natural wood are optional equipment at slight extra cost

It is the
TOP PLACE EIGHT
..in public acceptance as well as performance and value

1930 LINCOLN BRUNN BROUGHAM

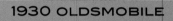

1930 OLDSMOBILE

Luxurious Transportation

All the treasures of ancient Egypt contributed to the splendor and luxury of Cleopatra's lavish barge

PACKARD luxury, once enjoyed, is seldom relinquished. Records indicate that 96% of all Packard owners remain in the family—replace their old Packards with new ones.

Packard has always been a luxury car. It has sought and found its patronage among those who know and appreciate fine things.

When such owners, after long, proud years of satisfaction, have come to part with their cars, they have naturally turned again to Packard. And Packard has always been ready with new and finer vehicles—improved mechani-

cally and more luxurious than ever, but retaining the characteristic beauty of style and design so distinctly Packard's own.

New customers, too, have turned to Packard when seeking supreme motor car luxury. Two-thirds of today's Packard Standard Eights are bought by those who give up other makes of cars.

What greater tribute to quality and reputation and engineering leadership can there be than that which old customers and new thus bestow on Packard? Act upon the Packard slogan and—

ASK THE MAN WHO OWNS ONE

PACKARD

PONTIAC BIG SIX

1930 PONTIAC BIG SIX FOUR-DOOR SEDAN

1930 PACKARD

NEW SERIES **PONTIAC BIG SIX**

1930 Pontiac Big Six Sport Coupe

1930 Pontiac

1930 Studebaker Commander

DISCOVER AMERICA
BEST BY CAR

1930 VIKING EIGHT

Cadillac V-8 prices range from $2695, f. o. b. Detroit—with G. M. A. C. terms available on all body types. The model illustrated below is the V-8 Town Sedan, with coachwork by Fisher.

1931 Chevrolet Six Convertible Cabriolet

For many years, the Cadillac Motor Car Company devoted all its energies to the perfection of a single product—the Cadillac V-8. Until 1927, Cadillac's entire reputation as a master builder was based upon this car. This fact has never been forgotten; and though the Cadillac line now includes three other distinguished cars — the La Salle, the V-12 and the V-16 — the V-8 is built, to this day, as if it were the sole protector of Cadillac's good name. In fact, no eight-cylinder Cadillac ever produced could compare with the present V-8. Yet, due to a vastly enlarged manufacturing program, this finest of V-8 Cadillacs is priced as low as $2695, f. o. b. Detroit.

1931 Cadillac V-8 Town Sedan

1931 Chevrolet Six DeLuxe Convertible Landau Phaeton

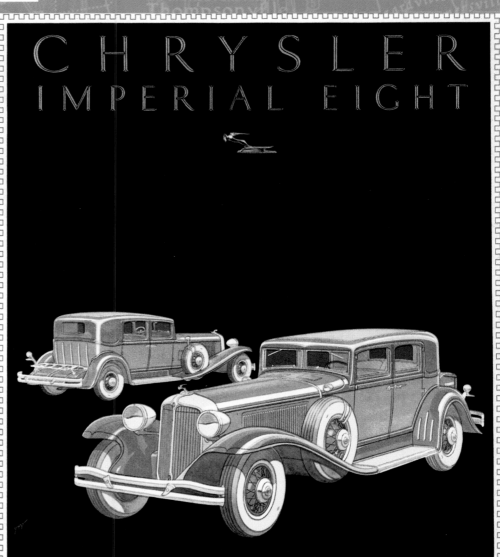

CHRYSLER
IMPERIAL EIGHT

1931 Chrysler Imperial Eight Close-Coupled Sedan

1931 Essex Super-Six Coach

HUDSON ESSEX

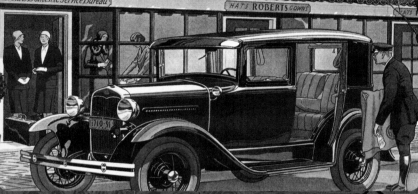

1931 Ford DeLux Sedan

1931 Ford Tudor Sedan

1931 General Motors

the

1931 HUDSON EIGHT SEDAN

1931 LINCOLN SEDAN

1931 LINCOLN

1931 OLDSMOBILE

1931 Oldsmobile

YOU'LL EXPERIENCE A FEELING OF UNUSUAL SECURITY WHEN YOU DRIVE THIS CAR

1931 Oldsmobile

FISHER has created bodies for the new Oldsmobile Six which are smartly styled and brightly finished in the sunny hues of spring, and which combine a wealth of comfort and a wide utility.

These bodies by Fisher are ready for the swift changes from sun to shower—ready with carefully-engineered, easily-operated window regulators and the Fisher vision-ventilating windshield. They are snugly insulated for the chilly day—instantly made cool and airy for the warmest weather.

Furthermore, Fisher wood-and-steel type construction provides Oldsmobile with bodies of greater

strength plus resilience—eliminates squeaks and rattles and assures comfort and good-looks through many seasons.

Be sure to examine carefully the new Oldsmobiles and compare their greater value. For in Oldsmobile's price field, the new Oldsmobile Six alone will give you these important Fisher superiorities, because Oldsmobile is one of the General Motors cars—the only cars with Body by Fisher.

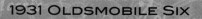

BODY FISHER
LOOK TO THE BODY

FISHER BODY CORPORATION · DETROIT, MICHIGAN
Division of General Motors

1931 Oldsmobile Six

WORLD SUPREMACY

China World-wide Packard preference is well typified in the Far East by the fine car registrations in the great city of Shanghai, China. There Packard cars outnumber—by more than two to one—all other makes of comparable price combined

1931 Packard Eight Sedan

riding comfort

P O N T I A C

1931 PONTIAC

1932 CHEVROLET SIX SPORT COUPE

As low as $475

SILENT
SYNCRO-MESH SHIFT

SIMPLIFIED
FREE WHEELING

IMPROVED
SIX-CYLINDER ENGINE

60 HORSEPOWER
(20% INCREASE)

65 TO 70 MILES AN HOUR

FASTER, QUIETER GETAWAY

SMOOTHER
OPERATION

SMARTER
FISHER BODIES

GREATER COMFORT
AND VISION

UNEQUALLED
ECONOMY

PRICED AS LOW AS

$475

All prices f.o.b. Flint, Mich. Special
equipment extra. Low delivered
prices and easy G.M.A.C. terms.

1932 CHEVROLET SIX STANDARD
FIVE-WINDOW COUPE

39

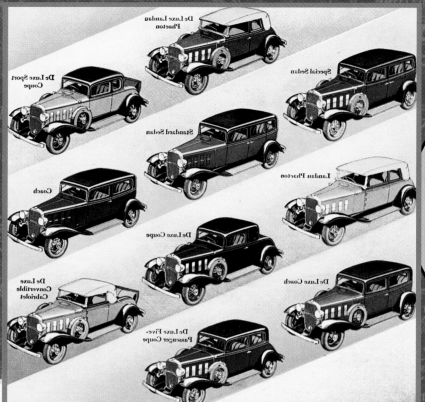

1932
CHEVROLET
SIX

1932
LINCOLN
CONVERTIBLE
SEDAN-
PHAETON

1932
LINCOLN
SEVEN-
PASSENGER
SEDAN

1932 Lincoln Two-Passenger Coupe

1932 Lincoln Seven-Passenger Sedan

1932 Lincoln Four-Passenger phaeton

1932 Oldsmobile Two-Door Sedan

1932 OLDSMOBILE

1932 OLDSMOBILE SIX AND STRAIGHT EIGHT

syncro mesh

NEW PONTIAC
SIXES and V-EIGHTS

1932 PONTIAC

It's spring

NEW

get a Pontiac . . .

PONTIAC 6 AND V-8

1932 PONTIAC SIX

1933 BUICK

1933 GENERAL MOTORS

1933 BUICK

1933 Oldsmobile Six and Straight Eight

1933 Oldsmobile Straight Eight and Six

Beauty

and comfort and performance combine to give fine car quality

1933 OLDSMOBILE EIGHT AND SIX

Beauty, comfort and performance . . . the three most desired motor car qualities . . . will be yours in *full* measure when you buy your new Master De Luxe Chevrolet for 1935. It is beautiful in *every* detail, with a beauty that only Fisher—the world's foremost builder of fine bodies—has learned how to build into a car. It is comfortable, too, for it has every improvement that modern engineering has developed to make your ride smooth—safe—pleasant. And in performance it will be a revelation to you. Because nobody has ever expected a builder of low-priced cars to build to the *finest* limits of precision manufacture, as Chevrolet builds this car. All these advantages combine to give fine car quality—the *highest* quality Chevrolet has ever offered . . . yet Chevrolet prices are low and Chevrolet operating economy is greater than ever before. May we suggest that you *prove* these facts by your own tests, and choose *Chevrolet* for quality at low cost.

CHEVROLET MOTOR COMPANY, DETROIT, MICHIGAN
Compare Chevrolet's low delivered prices and easy G.M.A.C. terms
A General Motors Value

CHEVROLET

The Master De Luxe Sport Coupe

1935 CHEVROLET

TURRET-TOP BODY BY FISHER (WITH FISHER VENTILATION SYSTEM) . . . IMPROVED KNEE-ACTION RIDE . . . BLUE-FLAME VALVE-IN-HEAD ENGINE . . . WEATHER-

1935 CHEVROLET MASTER DE LUXE SPORT COUPE

1936 Cadillac Fleetwood
Town Cabriolet

1936 Ford

1935 Lincoln Willoughby
Limousine

1936 Ford Four-Passenger
Club Cabriolet

Here's the car
Smart America is going for!

PRICED AS MUCH AS $300 LOWER!

$665 AND UP AT THE FACTORY

SMART TO BE SEEN IN...
SMARTER TO BUY

SOPHISTICATED in every lovely flowing line, this big, thrifty new 1936 Studebaker Champion is the world's first moderately priced car that's been deliberately designed to please your inherent good taste. You have gifted Helen Dryden, internationally famed stylist, to thank for that.

And with Studebaker prices now down as much as $300, you don't have to give a thought to one of the lowest priced cars . . . not this year. Just a few dollars more is all it takes to own this impressive new Champion with its unusual prestige and performance.

World's only car that won't roll back on a hill!
You won't find Studebaker's automatic hillholder in any other 1936 car. Indeed, with 97 featured advancements, including a thrilling money-saving automatic overdrive, this smart new Studebaker gives you more beauty, more comfort, more economy, more perform-

ance and more safety than you ever expected to get in any car whatever the price. Its luxurious, roomy interior is encased in the strongest and safest one-piece steel body in the world. It has feather-touch hydraulic brakes. And economy—it's almost shamelessly frugal with gasoline and oil.

Studebaker prices now begin as low as $665 for the new 90-horsepower Dictator . . . as low as $965 for the new 115-horsepower President. Studebaker's new C.I.T. 6% plan offers a new "low" in time payments.

NEW 1936 Studebaker

This Studebaker President cruising sedan trunk lights automatically when the lid is lifted at night. All Studebaker luggage compartments are exceptionally spacious and lock with a separate key.

1936 Studebaker

1937 Chevrolet

Vacation Days
are happier days when you go in a
CHEVROLET

Think how many places you can go . . . how many sights you will see . . . how many things you can do—if you take your vacation this summer in a Chevrolet! And think how comfortably you'll travel . . . how thrilling each mile will be . . . how little the trip will cost . . . in this smarter, safer, smoother-riding car! Vacation days are happier days when you go in a Chevrolet, because it's *free-handed* with thrills but a *miser* with its owner's money!

CHEVROLET MOTOR DIVISION, *General Motors Sales Corporation*
DETROIT, MICHIGAN

E ONLY COMPLETE CAR—PRICED SO LOW

1936 Hudson Terraplane

US
48

A CHEVROLET
is always good company

On short or long trips—in June or January—*wherever* and *whenever* you wish to go—you will find a Chevrolet the perfect traveling companion! Lively... instantly responsive to your every mood and desire... comfortable... and forever trustworthy. Own *the complete car, completely new*—the only low-priced car with all modern advantages—and you will agree it's always good company.

CHEVROLET MOTOR DIVISION, *General Motors Sales Corporation*, DETROIT, MICHIGAN

THE ONLY COMPLETE CAR · PRICED SO LOW

1937 CHEVROLET

SMARTEST CAR IN THE LOW-PRICE FIELD

1937 DeSoto

BY EVERY MODERN STANDARD THE FORD IS A BIG CAR

"Gee, Pop, I bet there'd be room for my bicycle too!"

1937 FORD

"But officer—when I told you I was just going to get a hat pretty enough for my new Ford, you said yourself THAT wouldn't be easy!"

DISTINCTIVE BEAUTY BORN OF USEFULNESS

Ford V·8

FOR 193

1937 FORD

1937 LINCOLN WILLOUGHBY LIMOUSINE

1937 LINCOLN LE BARON CONVERTIBLE ROADSTER

1937 OLDSMOBILE SIX AND EIGHT

OLDSMOBILE ANNOUNCE

A NEW SIX . . . A NEW EIGHT

THE DISTINCTIVE NEW OLDSMOBILE SIX for 1937 is different from anything else on the road . . . A striking new Style . . . A smashing new Value . . . The greatest new buy in the lower-price field . . . See it and you will see new and freshly original Style-Leader Styling— new and impressively bigger size and roominess—new safety with fleetness and smoothness— a new all-time value-high, even for Oldsmobile! . . . Outstanding among its newest advantages is the new Unisteel Turret Top Body by Fisher . . . A bigger new Oldsmobile six-cylinder engine gives it new power-brilliance with newly increased economy . . . Look at its superlative quality—look at its low price—and your choice is sure to be this great new Oldsmobile Six.

Each with a Style Distinctly its Own!

FRESH, NEW STYLE-LEADER STYLING
LONGER WHEELBASE · LARGER SIZE
ROOMIER BODIES · LOWER FLOORS
WIDER CHASSIS · HEAVIER FRAMES
BIGGER ENGINES · HIGHER POWER
EXTRA SAFETY · GREATER ECONOMY
AND OLDSMOBILE'S TRADITIONALLY
FINE QUALITY

NEW UNISTEEL TURRET TOP BODIES BY
FISHER · NEW COMPLETELY SEALED
SUPER-HYDRAULIC BRAKES · CENTER-
CONTROL STEERING · NEW DUAL
RIDE STABILIZERS, FRONT AND REAR
PROVED KNEE-ACTION WHEELS
SMOOTH UNOBSTRUCTED FLOORS · AND
MANY OTHERS

The Cars that have Everything for 1937

THE DISTINGUISHED NEW OLDSMOBILE EIGHT for 1937 marks a thrill-
achievement . . . A new conception of fine-car Luxury . . . A definite new
car Value . . . The truly fine car of popular price . . . See it and you will
more commanding car—a roomier and more luxurious car—the real Styl
fine-car field! . . . With its new Unisteel Turret Top Body by Fisher, it
convenient and more comfortable than ever . . . With its bigger, smoothe
engine, it is more powerful, more flexible, more responsive . . . For those
the finest, the 1937 Oldsmobile Eight—at its moderate price—is the year

Think Twice of their Safety!

No other car in the world can give you all of Oldsmobile's famous safety features. Oldsmobile originated the Safety Instrument Unit which groups all instruments on a direct line of vision before the driver's eyes. Oldsmobile developed and introduced the Automatic Safety Transmission which provides greater flexibility and simplified car control. In addition, Oldsmobile offers a score of other safety advantages—including Safety Dash, Safety Interiors, Knee-Action Wheels, Center-Control Steering, Super-Hydraulic Brakes and Unisteel Turret Top Body by Fisher with Safety Glass. Think of *Safety* first when you select your new car—and you'll think first of Oldsmobile.

THE EIGHT

NOWHERE ELSE CAN MONEY BUY SO MUCH!

Style-Leader Styling • Safety Dash with Safety Instrument Unit • Safety Interiors • 95-Horsepower Six • 110-Horsepower Eight Knee-Action Wheels • Super-Hydraulic Brakes • Center-Control Steering • Unisteel Body by Fisher • No Draft Ventilation

Automatic Safety Transmission—Optional at Extra Cost

THE SIX

New Safety Instrument Unit with Safety Dash Controls, speedometer and gauges are grouped in a single clearly viewed unit directly in front of the driver. The dash is free from sharp projecting knobs and handles. The car illustrated is equipped with the Automatic Safety Transmission . . . optional at extra cost on all 1938 models.

Step Ahead and Be Money Ahead!
DRIVE AN
Oldsmobile
A GENERAL MOTORS VALUE

1938 OLDSMOBILE

THE 4-DOOR SEDAN

THE 4-DOOR CONVERTIBLE SEDAN

1937 PONTIAC

Step out Ahead in Quality and Style!

WITH THE greatest roll call of features ever provided in cars of popular price . . . with styling that is setting the trend for all America to follow . . . the 1938 Oldsmobiles offer motorists the opportunity of a lifetime. Now you can enjoy a Style-Leading car . . . a pace-setting car . . . a quality car . . . at costs that are extremely moderate. And in the light of what you get for what you pay, you will be saving money every mile!

LOOKING FOR THE LOW-PRICED CAR with THE MOST NEW FEATURES?

Pontiac's the Answer!

AMERICA'S FINEST LOW-PRICED CAR

1938 PONTIAC SILVER-STREAKED

YOUR MONEY NEVER BOUGHT SO MUCH!

Style-Leader Styling • Safety Dash with Safety Instrument Unit • Safety Interiors • 95-Horsepower Six • 110-Horsepower Eight • Knee-Action Wheels • Super-Hydraulic Brakes • Center-Control Steering • Unisteel Body by Fisher • Turret Top • Under-Hood Battery • No Draft Ventilation • Safety Glass • Unobstructed Floors • Weather Sealed Doors • Dual Ride Stabilizers • Electro-Hardened Aluminum Pistons Scientific Sound Proofing • Big, Low-Pressure Tires • Insulated Body

Automatic Safety Transmission—the New Driving Sensation— Optional at Extra Cost on All Models of Both Six and Eight.

AUTOMATIC SAFETY TRANSMISSION!

Step Ahead and Be Money Ahead! DRIVE AN
Oldsmobile

1938 OLDSMOBILE

" I heard on the party line you had a new Ford, but sakes alive, I didn't think you'd bring it out here 'til the spring thaw was over! "

1939 FORD V-8 TUDOR SEDAN

1939 FORD

or Company
fers
ITY CARS

RY   LINCOLN-ZEPHYR   LINCOLN

lovely that I haven't a thing to go with it!"

do hope your new Ford arrives by daylight!

1939 FORD DE LUXE FORDOR SEDAN

This is the De Luxe Fordor Sedan in Jefferson Blu

Its very bigness is a big surprise!

1939 FORD DE LUXE FORDOR SEDAN

1939 LINCOLN-ZEPHYR V-12

1939 LINCOLN-ZEPHYR V-12

1939 LINCOLN-ZEPHYR V-12

1939 LINCOLN-ZEPHYR V-12

MERCURY 8
A PRODUCT OF THE FORD MOTOR COMPANY

1939 MERCURY 8

MERCURY V8 TYPE
A PRODUCT OF THE FORD MOTOR COMPANY

1939 MERCURY 8

PLYMOUTH'S THE CAR!

"So Beautiful You Won't Believe It's a Low-Priced Car!"

GLAMOROUS NEW DISTINCTION IN STYLING...Lavish New Luxury...Longer Wheelbase...New High-Torque Engine Performance...Perfected Remote Control Shifting with New All-Silent Auto-Mesh Transmission ...New Amola Steel Coil Springs...New "Safety Signal" Speedometer.

PERFECTED REMOTE CONTROL GEAR SHIFT

THE BEAUTIFUL NEW PLYMOUTH FOR 1939 now on display at your nearby Plymouth dealer. See it, ride in it, drive it, today!

NEW "SAFETY SIGNAL" SPEEDOMETER

Indicator Light shows green up to 30 miles per hour...from 30 to 50, amber ...above 50, a warning red.

A NEW "ROADKING"...AND A NEW "DE LUXE"...GREAT NEW VALUES!

SEE what it is that *makes* Plymouth the car of the year: New, sweeping lines, the last word in style...new design headlamps giving greatly increased road lighting...new luxury interiors, great roominess!

Ride in this great Plymouth...drive it and experience the soft, new riding ease of its new Amola Steel Coil Springs, patented Floating Power engine mountings and 100% hydraulic, double-action brakes.

New True-Steady steering requires 15% less effort. Clutch and brake pedal pressure have been reduced. This new Plymouth is the *easiest-handling car you ever drove!*

And for 1939, Plymouth has thrilling new High-Torque engine performance...with *new* all-round economy!

Remarkably easy to own...your present car will probably represent a large proportion of Plymouth's low delivered price...balance in surprisingly low monthly instalments. See your nearby Plymouth dealer today. PLYMOUTH DIVISION OF CHRYSLER CORPORATION, Detroit, Michigan.

THIS YEAR PLYMOUTH'S THE CAR

PLYMOUTH BUILDS GREAT CARS

1939 PLYMOUTH

PLYMOUTH "ROADKING" 5-PASSENGER SEDAN

$685

—"Detroit delivered price," including front and rear bumpers and bumper guards, spare wheel, tire and tube, foot control for headlight beam with indicator on instrument panel, ash-tray front and rear, sun visor, safety glass and big trunk space (19.3 cubic feet). Plymouth "Roadking" models start at $645; "De Luxe" models slightly higher. Plymouth prices INCLUDE ALL FEDERAL TAXES. State, local taxes not included.

TUNE IN MAJOR BOWES' ORIGINAL AMATEUR HOUR... COLUMBIA NETWORK, THURS., 9 TO 10 P. M., E. S. T.

GET A CHEVROLET

1940 Ford

The Special De Luxe Sport Sedan, $802*

and *GET AWAY FIRST!*

1940 Chevrolet Special De Luxe Sport Sedan

1940 Mercury 8

Alive with Innovations!

1940 DODGE *with NEW FULL-FLOATING RIDE*

1940 Dodge

Out of the World's Greatest Plant

THE NEW FORD CARS ARE ROLLING

1940 Ford De Luxe Fordor Sedan

1940 Hudson Six

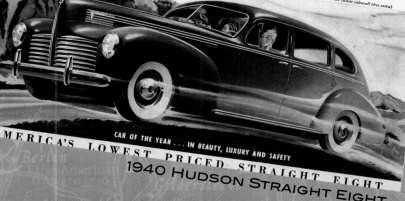

1940 Lincoln-Zephyr V-12

1940 Hudson Straight Eight

LINCOLN ZEPHYR *V-12*

1940 LINCOLN-ZEPHYR V-12S

1940 MERCURY 8

1940 Packard One-Twenty Touring Sedan

1940 Oldsmobile

1940 Mercury 8

"Someday *I'll* own a Car Like that"

1940 Plymouth Convertible Coupe

"...I Can Go just Where I Please!"

1940 PLYMOUTH

Special Six 4-Door Touring Sedan, $884*
There's superlative comfort in its wide seats and "Triple-Cushioned" ride

Special Six Sport Coupe, $827*
Has a full-width, full-cushioned rear seat for occasion
(This model also available in De Luxe Six and De Luxe Eight)

It's Spring - and Summe
- Pick Out You

De Luxe Eight 2-Door Touring Sedan, $919*
(And there's an equally charming De Luxe Six 2-Door Sedan)

De Luxe Six 4-Door Touring Sedan, $940*
Two-tone finish as illustrated available
on any Pontiac model at no extra cost
(Same model on De Luxe Eight chassis priced slightly higher)

De Luxe Six Cabriolet, $1011*
Colored upholstery in leather or leather and whipcord—
to harmonize with body and top colors
(This model also available on De Luxe Eight chassis)

1940 PONTIAC

Listen - a Pontiac is being sold!

'Come on — you're going to get the thrill of your lives! I'm going to take you home in that big, beautiful new Pontiac of mine!

"What! A new Pontiac? Sort of putting on the Ritz, aren't you?"

"Not a bit of it. Pontiac costs a lot less than you think — and my gasoline bills are the lowest ever."

"Well, you really have me interested. What dealer did you buy it from?"

MOST PONTIAC owners are that way! They seldom miss an opportunity to say a good word about their cars.

Of course, this is the most effective salesmanship in the world. When an owner tells a friend, the recommendation goes a long way. In fact, our owners sell thousands of cars for us every year.

Why do they do this? Because they like the easy way Pontiac handles. They like its beauty — its comfort — its safety — its performance — and its generous size. And, above all, they like its economy.

If you're thinking about a new car, why don't you talk with any Pontiac owner? You're certain to hear an interesting story.

Special Six 4-Door Touring Sedan, as Illustrated $876*

Help promote Safety—
Dim your lights when passing

$783 FOR THE SPECIAL SIX BUSINESS COUPE
(OTHER MODELS SLIGHTLY HIGHER)
*Delivered at Pontiac, Mich. Transportation based on rail rates, state and local taxes (if any), optional equipment and accessories—extra. Prices subject to change without notice. General Motors terms to suit your purse.

Pontiac
AMERICA'S FINEST LOW-PRICED CAR

1940 PONTIAC SPECIAL SIX FOUR-
DOOR TOURING SEDAN

AUTOMATIC CANNON
FOR THE AIR CORPS!

The cannon are comin
They're rolling 'em off Old
mobile's production lines rig
now — automatic cannon for fightin
planes. In addition, high-caliber she
for the field artillery are being turne
out in Oldsmobile's manufacturin
arsenal at the rate of thousands a da

AUTOMATIC DRIVES for the B-44

BETTER LOOKING,
BETTER LASTING, BETTER BUIL
THAN ANY OLDS IN 44 YEARS

HYDRA-MATIC

NO CLUTCH TO PRESS!

NO GEARS TO SHIFT!

AVES 10 TO 15% ON GAS!

As AN "all-out" aid to driving efficiency, Hydra-Matic* has no equal. For only Hydra-Matic is completely automatic. It eliminates the clutch pedal — and hence, all clutch pushing. It banishes all manual gear shifting in the four forward speeds. It saves time, conserves energy and reduces gasoline consumption by 10 to 15 per cent. And it smooths out and steps up performance. Hydra-Matic Drive is offered in all models of the new Olds B-44, the car that's stamina-styled and stamina-built to meet the new tempo of the times. Try automatic Hydra-Matic in the

B-44 today—the 100 H. P. Six or the 110 H. P. Eight. You'll be pleased with the quality of the car and you'll like Hydra-Matic, automatically!

★ DEFENSE COMES FIRST ★
WITH OLDSMOBILE!

Defense takes full priority at Oldsmobile. Production of cannon and shell gets preference in plant facilities and man power. In addition, Oldsmobile is setting up for still further defense assignments. Meanwhile, Oldsmobile's remaining resources are devoted to building the new Olds B-44 — building it in limited quantity, to release vital materials for our country's armament needs.

OU CAN ALWAYS COUNT ON

OLDSMOBILE

*Optional at Extra Cost

It's Quality-Built
to last!

1941 OLDSMOBILE

ust Around the Corner

Pontiac!

Special Six 2-Door Touring Sedan, $830*
g, luxurious Pontiac sedan priced right down with the lowest

*Special Six Business Coupe, $783**
Built for extra-rugged service and lowest operating cost

*De Luxe Six Business Coupe, $835**
(Pontiac also builds the Business Coupe on the De Luxe Eight chassis)

*"orpedo" Eight 4-Door Touring Sedan, $1092**
*Acknowledged Leader of the 1940 Style Parade!
wo-tone finish as illustrated optional on any Pontiac model
at slight extra cost)*

IT'S AN OLD, and exciting, American custom to meet Spring more than halfway in a fresh, sparkling, new motor car.

To help you make your 1940 Spring selection, Pontiac portrays on these pages eleven of its seventeen 1940 models.

It will make you feel better all over to take to the road in one of these big, wide-seated, long-wheelbase beauties—especially after driving a smaller car. Feel the smoothness of that power-packed Pontiac engine. Feel the comfort of that Pontiac "Triple-Cushioned" ride. And enjoy the luxury that surrounds you in Pontiac's "big car" interior.

And when you get a check on the economy of operating a Pontiac, you'll really begin to realize what a marvelous car you've bought. For records prove that Pontiac issues a very defiant economy challenge to even the smallest cars.

The biggest thrill, of course, is the Pontiac price. It's in easy reach of everyone, *right down with the lowest!*

*Delivered at Pontiac, Mich. Transportation based on rail rates, state and local taxes (if any), optional equipment and accessories—extra. Prices subject to change without notice. General Motors terms to suit your purse.

His dad took his advice !

"Yes sir—my Dad did just what I told him to! I said—'Gee, Dad, why don't we get a big car this time?'

"I said—'Let's get a Pontiac and step up in the world!' At first, he thought a Pontiac would cost too much. But I had the figures all ready for him.

"As soon as he found out how low-priced a Pontiac is, the rest was easy! He just took one look at that car—and he bought it in about five minutes!"

*Special Six 4-Door Touring Sedan, as illustrated $876**

A GENERAL MOTORS VALUE

WELL, SONNY, you gave your Dad some good advice. It's very sensible to buy a Pontiac. It's big —it's beautiful—it's safe—and it's comfortable. And it's priced right down with the lowest. ¶ Yes, it's small wonder that America is picking Pontiac in ever-increasing quantities. When you can get a car so good and so big and so beautiful—at a price so low—it doesn't take the average buyer long to make up his mind. ¶ Are you buying a car this spring? If so, better make it a Pontiac.

ONLY
$783
FOR THE
SPECIAL SIX
BUSINESS
COUPE
OTHER MODELS
SLIGHTLY HIGHER

Pontiac
AMERICA'S FINEST LOW-PRICED CAR

*Delivered at Pontiac, Michigan. Transportation based on rail rates, state and local taxes (if any), optional equipment and accessories—extra. Prices are subject to change without notice.

1940 PONTIAC SPECIAL SIX FOUR-DOOR
TOURING SEDAN

Special De Luxe
SPORT SEDAN
Also available in the Master De Luxe Series

Look at CHEVROLET'S '41 line and you'll say
"FIRST BECAUSE IT'S FINEST!"

1941 CHEVROLET

POWER LIKE NIAGARA'S ...WITH TURBINE SMOOTHNESS!

TRY *Chrysler Fluid Drive*
WITH VACAMATIC TRANSMISSION !

1941 CHRYSLER

THE SMARTNESS OF A COUPE !

THE ROOMINESS OF A SEDAN !

The Chrysler six-passenger Convertible Club Coupe

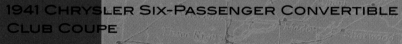

1941 CHRYSLER SIX-PASSENGER CONVERTIBLE
CLUB COUPE

Why Dream it?... Drive it !

1941 DESOTO DE LUXE TWO-DOOR SEDAN

$825†

1941 DODGE

A FLUID DRIVING SUMMER

thanks to **Dodge**

SMOOTHEST CARS AFLOAT—

ITS ship, ship AHOY—and anchors aweigh, as you too become the happy master and skipper of a Dodge Propeller-Driven Cruiser. Here are the smoothest things afloat on any highway. The sleekest in any traffic. The lowest priced and the fastest-selling cars with Fluid Drive in all the world. This means that your own good buying judgment has already been confirmed a hundred thousand times and more—by other brand-new Captains of these Dodge Fluid Drive Cruisers. ¶ They'll tell you it's a new day in motorcars, and you might better be in on it while these Dodge prices last and drive forevermore without constant clutching and shifting as of old. Your foot now does tirelessly almost all the things your arms and body used to do in ordinary cars. The daintiest slipper, too, will command these power-giants, and they'll behave for "her" like handsome, well-trained servants.

SAFETY-RIM WHEELS
GUARD YOUR TIRES AND YOU

FULL-FLOATING RIDE
FOR A "RIDING ZONE" WITH COMPLETE SHOCK PROTECTION

FLOATING POWER
ENGINE MOUNTINGS CRADLE YOUR ENGINE FOR LONG LIFE

SAFETY-STEEL BODY
FOR MAXIMUM SAFETY AND YOUR PEACE OF MIND

MASTER HYDRAULIC BRAKES
FOR EQUAL-PRESSURE BRAKING EFFICIENCY AND SAFETY

DODGE FLUID DRIVE
DRIVING BECOMES GLIDING AS YOU RULE THE ROAD

FINGER-TIP STEERING
FOR SWEETER, SMOOTHER HANDLING AT THE WHEEL

ALL-FLUID DRIVE *Dodge*

FLUID DRIVE $25 EXTRA

Car Prices Subject to Change Without Notice

1941 DODGE

1941 FORD

1941 LINCOLN-ZEPHYR V-12

1941 FORD

1941 LINCOLN-ZEPHYR V-12

Look Out For Those Clouds !

1941 LINCOLN-ZEPHYR V-12

Gosh, The Folks All Love Me !

1941 LINCOLN-ZEPHYR V-12

1941 LINCOLN-ZEPHYR V-12

SHIFTS ITS OWN GEARS!

Drive an Olds Hydra-Matic and you'll experience thrills that you've never known before. Shifting through all four forward speeds is entirely *automatic!*

ELIMINATES THE CLUTCH COMPLETELY!

You never push a clutch pedal—because there's no clutch in the car. You drive with your right foot *alone*—using accelerator and brake pedal only!

PROVIDES A SPECIAL "PICK-UP" GEAR

You cruise in super-smooth "fourth"—but if you want a quick burst of power, you simply press through on the accelerator and a special pick-up gear sweeps you ahead like magic!

GIVES MATCHLESS ACCELERATION!

You get away from a standing start with *full* accelerating power. You glide through the four forward speeds in a twinkling. Gears are always in mesh. There's no lag in the changes!

DOES THINGS NO OTHER "DRIVE" CAN DO!

HYDRA-MATIC DRIVE*

Hydra-Matic Drive is the *only* "drive" that combines fluid coupling and a completely automatic four-speed transmission. It cuts *down* driving effort and steps *up* performance. All you do is drive is step on it, steer and stop!

Custom Cruiser 4-Door Sedan—Six, $1099—Eight, $1135*. White side-wall tires extra.*

Drive an Oldsmobile Hydra-Matic and you enjoy advantages no other "drive" can give you! Advantages in responsiveness, flexibility, performance and ease of operation. Hydra-Matic Drive is offered on *all* Oldsmobile models, both Sixes and Eights—the low-priced Olds Special, the stunning Dynamic Cruiser and the luxurious Custom Cruiser! For a new and different thrill—take a Hydra-Matic drive today!

PRICES BEGIN AT $852* FOR SPECIAL SIX BUSINESS COUPE

Sedan prices begin at $898. *delivered at Lansing, Mich. Prices include Safety Glass, Bumpers, Spare Wheel, Tire, Tube, Dual Horns, 2 Windshield Wipers, 2 Sun Visors. State tax, optional equipment and accessories—extra. Prices subject to change without notice. A GENERAL MOTORS VALUE

*Optional at extra cost

STYLED TO LEAD BUILT TO LAST

THE CAR *Ahead!* IT'S **OLDSMOBILE** WITH HYDRA-MATIC DRIVE*!

1941 Oldsmobile
Custom Cruiser
Four-Door Sedan

The Car Ahead! It's OLDSMOBILE!

STYLED TO LEAD BUILT TO LAST

6 NEW LINES FOR '41
3 SIXES 3 EIGHTS

ALL offering HYDRA-MATIC DRIVE

NEWEST and *newest* of all the new cars for 1941 is the beautiful big new Oldsmobile! *NEW* wider choice of cars!—the biggest, broadest line in Oldsmobile history. *NEW* ultra-modern *Style!*—stunning new front ends, new wing-type fenders, massive new dreadnaught-design bumpers. *NEW ultra-modern Fisher bodies!*—three distinct types of advanced streamlining, a style for every taste. *NEW* imposing *length* and *bigness!*—longer wheelbases, wider rear treads, wider rear seats, roomier interiors. *NEW bigger higher-powered engines!*—the Econo-Master Six stepped up to 100 Horsepower, the Straight Eight again 110 Horsepower. *NEW* interior luxury and richness!—finer upholstery, appointments and conveniences. *NEW* innovations and special features!—including the last word in ventilating and heating systems (available at extra cost)—Oldsmobile's sensational and exclusive "Condition-Air." And with all these new advancements, scores of proved Oldsmobile features, such as modern coil springs all around, that are still NEWS to millions. The car to see first for '41 is "the car ahead"—it's Oldsmobile, now on nation-wide display!

NO CLUTCH NO SHIFT!

Crowning all Oldsmobile advancements for 1941 is Hydra-Matic Drive—Olds' exclusive combination of fluid coupling and completely automatic transmission. With no clutch and no shift, it simplifies driving, steps up performance, saves gas. It's optional at extra cost. Try it *now!*

NEW DYNAMIC CRUISER (shown in red) 125-inch wheelbase. Two body types. Six or eight-cylinder power. Popular price.

NEW CUSTOM CRUISER (shown in blue) 125-inch wheelbase. Four body types. Six or eight-cylinder power. Medium price.

NEW OLDS SPECIAL (shown in yellow) 119-inch wheelbase. Six body types. Six or eight-cylinder power. Low price.

THE CAR THAT HAS EVERYTHING *Modern!*

1941 Oldsmobile

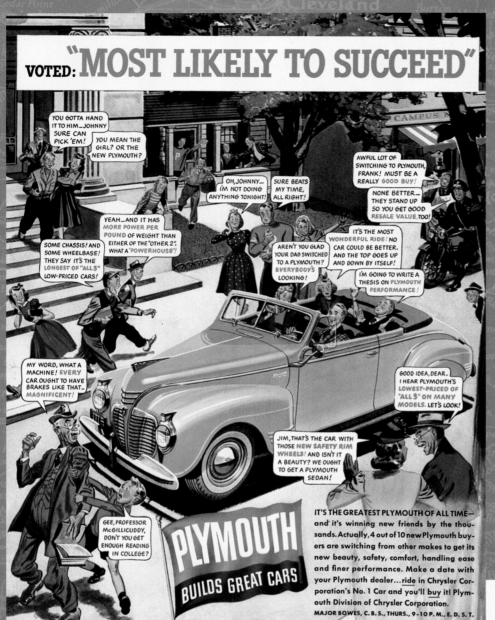

1941 Plymouth

1941 Pontiac

A STEP
in the right direction

Streamliner "Torpedo" Six Sedan Coupe, $923* (white sidewall tires extra)

1941 OLDSMOBILE CUSTOM
CRUISER FOUR-DOOR SEDAN

"Come on, Gang! Now we've got
something to *Crow* about!"

De Luxe "Torpedo" Six Business Coupe $828* (white sidewall tires extra)

YES, INDEED, you have *plenty* to crow about when a handsome, new Pontiac "Torpedo," comes into your family. No one can blame you, either, for this big, gleaming beauty proves that you know what's *right* in motor car styles. And in comfort, too. In Pontiac's roomy body by Fisher, you and your friends will find comfort beyond compare.

YOU CAN CROW, also, about how little it costs you to drive your new Pontiac "Torpedo," if you like. Pontiac has long been recognized as one of America's most economical cars and, in spite of their increased size and power, 1941 models match earlier Pontiacs in gasoline and oil economy and freedom from need for repairs.

AS FOR SAFETY, dependability, handling ease and the other qualities you want, thousands of owners of new Pontiacs consider their cars the equals in all respects of other cars costing hundreds of dollars more. Yet *Pontiac prices are so close to the lowest that if you can afford any new car you can afford a new Pontiac "Torpedo."*

A GENERAL MOTORS MASTERPIECE

THE *FINE* CAR

Pontiac
WITH THE LOW PRICE

ONLY $25 MORE FOR AN EIGHT IN ANY MODEL

PONTIAC PRICES BEGIN AT $828 FOR DE LUXE "TORPEDO" SIX BUSINESS COUPE

*Delivered at Pontiac, Mich. State tax, optional equipment and accessories—extra. Prices subject to change without notice

1941 PONTIAC DE LUXE "TORPEDO"
SIX BUSINESS COUPE

"Torpedo EVERYBODY!"

3 Great New "Torpedo" Lines
The De Luxe · The Streamliner · The Custom
with your choice of a Six or an Eight in any model

PONTIAC'S THREE brilliant new lines of cars for 1941 start with the De Luxe "Torpedoes"—five big, handsome models at prices which any new car buyer can afford.

Next in line come the Streamliner "Torpedoes," slightly larger, strikingly different and only a little higher in cost.

The array is completed by the Custom "Torpedoes," including the popular Station Wagon, which, in view of all the luxuries they offer, are very reasonably priced.

And any one of the models shown—any 1941 Pontiac, in fact—is available either as a six or an eight, with the eight only $25 more than the six.

Thus, it is actually true that now there's a Pontiac "Torpedo" for everybody—from owners of lowest-priced cars to those accustomed to buying in the higher brackets.

A visit to your nearest Pontiac dealer will reward you with detailed information about the automobile industry's number one value for 1941.

It's Another Big Year for Pontiac!

AMERICA'S FINEST LOW-PRICED CAR

A GENERAL MOTORS VALUE

COUPE

TREAMLINER "TORPEDO" FOUR-DOOR SEDAN

TREAMLINER "TORPEDO" SEDAN COUPE

CUSTOM "TORPEDO" SEDAN COUPE

1941 LINCOLN ZEPHYR V-12

...so nice to come home to!

BUY MORE WAR BONDS

BUY STILL MORE WAR BONDS

...ghting isn't over. Nor is Buick's war ...shed.

...ry in Europe is releasing many fighting

The roads are here. The days come with each rising sun. And the bustle that now enlivens Buick's factories is the make-ready process for ...

This is the 1942 Buick which sets the high standards to be surpassed in new models now being made ready.

WHEN BETTER AUTOMOBILES ARE BUILT

BUICK

1941 BUICK

The Finest Lincolns Ever Built

1942 LINCOLN-ZEPHYR V-12

1942 DeSoto

The Finest Lincolns Ever Built

1942 LINCOLN-ZEPHYR V-12

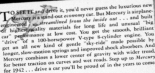

1942 Mercury 8

1942 Oldsmobiles

Fighters flying for victory—powered by Chevrolet-built Pratt & Whitney engines

Bombers now over the target—powered by Chevrolet-built Pratt & Whitney engines

Cargo planes ferrying men and matériel—powered by Chevrolet-built Pratt & Whitney engines

90-mm. guns for anti-tank and anti-aircraft use—built by Chevrolet

Armored cars spearheading Allied advances—built by Chevrolet

Millions of shells now blasting the enemy on all fronts—built by Chevrolet

*These illustrations reproduced from official U. S. Army Signal Corps photographs

Hundreds of thousands of military trucks aiding our fighting men everywhere—built by Chevrolet

Countless aluminum forgings serving in practically every type of warplane—produced by Chevrolet

1945 Chevrolet

The Best Car the Leader Ever Built — FEATURING distinguished new styling, new colors, new exterior and interior ornamentation, plus many other important extra values that will cause you to say— "CHEVROLET IS FIRST AGAIN!"

1946 Chevrolet

Style PAGE from tomorrow's Book

USA 1946

WHEN

1946 Buick

"CHEVROLET IS FIRST AGAIN!"

Wise Buyers are saying "CHEVROLET IS FIRST AGAIN!"

First in Quality at Low Prices

1946 CHEVROLET

1946 CHEVROLET

CHEVROLET *The Nation's Number 1 Car*

1st in Sales
during 10 of the last 11 car-production years

1st in Total Registrations
1 out of every 4 cars in use is a Chevrolet

1st in Owner Loyalty
among all lowest-priced cars, according to three impartial nationwide surveys

1946 CHEVROLET

1946 DODGE

A triumph in smart motor cars

"TOWN AND COUNTRY"... a Chrysler
original... a new concept in car design to link your
worlds of work and play. Another product of
Chrysler's advanced and resourceful engineering.

1946 CHRYSLER TOWN AND COUNTRY

33

Ford's out Front in *style*, too!

The Big New 1946 Ford Sedan Coupe

You have never seen a more beautiful instrument panel! And you've never seen a more colorful two-toned interior than you'll find in this luxurious new Ford!

There's a
Ford
in your future

Whatever model you choose, the big new 1946 Ford
car is a streamlined beauty from the newly styled
grille to the rugged rear bumper! And there's re-
freshing new elegance inside, too. Rich fabrics
Restful seats! A new instrument panel, smartly
decorated with plastic trim! For performance, Ford
is the only car in the low-priced field with a 100 h.p.
V-type, 8-cylinder engine (the type used in America's costliest cars) ... the only car that gives you
the safety of such big, oversized, self-centering, hydraulic brakes! See it at your Ford dealer's today!

TUNE IN { The FORD-Bob Crosby Show—CBS, Wednesdays, 9:30-10 P. M., E.S.T.
The FORD Sunday Evening Hour—ABC, Sundays, 8-9 P. M., E.S.T.

1946 DODGE

1946 FORD COUPE

FORD'S OUT FRONT
with *Headline Features!*

FORD ALONE GIVES YOU A CHOICE OF TWO GREAT ENGINES!
Only Ford offers you the 100 h.p. V-8 engine . . . the smoothest, liveliest engine in the low-priced field . . . or the brilliant 90 h.p. Six! Here's performance for every need! And for economy, both the V-8 and the Six are thriftier than ever, thanks to new 4-ring aluminum pistons and new balanced carburetion.

FORD ALONE HAS "KING-SIZED" BRAKES . . .
the biggest brakes in the low-priced field . . . the oversized hydraulics that could stop a car of twice the weight. They're self-centering, too, for faster, smoother, safer stops on any surface!

FORD ALONE HAS THE "LIFEGUARD" BODY . . .
with heavy-gauge steel and all-welded unit construction for super-safety. The "Lifeguard" body has special phosphate coating, anti-rust protection of *all* sheetmetal body parts, plus a long-lasting baked-enamel finish that's another "Ford First" . . . it "keeps that showroom complexion!"

There's a *Ford* in your future

"The liveliest performer in the low-priced field"

"King-sized brakes"

"That best-dressed look!"

"Rest-Ride springs!"

"Extra large trunk... that's no joke, son!"

Ford's out Front
WITH EVERYBODY!

"Wide-angle vision!"

"Lifeguard body!"

"Aye, and thrifty, too!"

"A roomy, two-tone interior!"

There's a *Ford* in your future

"A wise buy!"

FORD'S OUT FRONT
with the *young-in-heart!*

THERE'S A *Ford* IN YOUR FUTURE

Ford is the only car in its class with 100 horsepower and the V-type, 8-cylinder engine!

When people look at the new 1946 Ford Convertible, they say: "It's a *honey!*"

When they touch the top-raising button, they say: "It's a *sedan* in 30 seconds!"

When they drive the big new 100 horsepower V-8 engine, they say: "It's the liveliest thing on wheels!"

See your friendly Ford dealer and give him your order for a Ford Convertible . . . the car that's smart for the young-in-heart.

TUNE IN . . . The FORD-Bob Crosby Show—CBS, Wednesdays, 9:30-10 p. m., E. S. T.
The FORD Sunday Evening Hour—ABC, Sundays, 8-9 p. m., E. S. T.

1946 FORDS

1946 Hudson

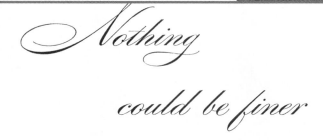
1946 Hudson Commodore Sedan

ONE LOOK TELLS YOU...

1946 Lincoln

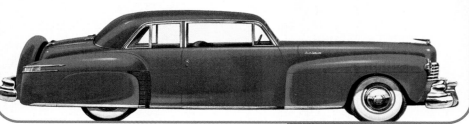

Nothing

could be finer

1946 Lincoln Continental
Coupe

Nothing

could be finer

1946 Lincoln Continental
Cabriolet

1946 LINCOLN

Nothing could be finer

More OF EVERYTHING YOU WANT WITH Mercury

SPORT-STYLED COZINESS Take the wheel of a new Mercury, and the question changes from *what car shall I buy* to *which Mercury model suits me best!* Here's one answer—the Sedan Coupe—with the coziness and sport styling of a coupe and roominess of a sedan. Flexible in traffic, it seems to spread wings on the highway . . . a big, lively car with more of everything you want!

MORE LUXURY Open these extra-wide doors . . . here's spaciousness that'll surprise you! Deep rear seat holds three. Front seats pivot inward for easy entrance and exit. Rich two-tone interiors. Here's smartness all the way through!

MORE STORAGE SPACE You'll find greater luggage room than you'd believe possible. You can take along *all* those extra bags . . . for more comfort and convenience. Truly, Mercury gives you more of everything!

MORE ROADABILITY Click off miles by the hundreds . . . you'll arrive fresh and rested in a Mercury. This car is built for the road, it's steady—sure—easy to handle, thanks to two-way stabilization and balanced weight. More fun to drive . . . that's Mercury!

— MERCURY — DIVISION OF FORD MOTOR COMPANY —

TUNE IN . . . FORD-Bob Crosby Show . . . CBS, Wed., 9.30-10 p.m., E.S.T. The FORD Sunday Evening Hour . . . ABC, Sundays, 8-9 p.m., E.S.T.

1946 MERCURY

MORE STORAGE SPACE
The extra trunk space of a coupe is combined with the seating capacity of a sedan in this Mercury sedan-coupe. Seats six people easily—with room to spare—and holds all the luggage you want.

MORE COMFORT
Roomy and restful! Doors are extra wide; front seats swivel inward; door controls are set forward so children in rear seat can't touch them—all examples of carefully planned Mercury details.

MORE MILEAGE
Balanced carburetion means peak efficiency at all speeds. Moreover, your Mercury engine makes fewer revolutions per minute while supplying its famous pickup and power; *less fuel, less wear.*

More OF EVERYTHING YOU WANT WITH Mercury

It's *more car for the money*—this new Mercury beauty. More graceful than ever, more luxurious, livelier . . . lots more satisfying in every way—with more improvements than would ordinarily be included in yearly models! New two-tone interiors in a choice of colors. New riding smoothness, new flexibility, even peppier performance. You'll agree, *you get more of everything with Mercury!*

MERCURY—DIVISION OF FORD MOTOR COMPANY

TUNE IN
The FORD-Bob Crosby Show . . . CBS, Wednesdays, 9.30-10 p.m., E.D.S.T.
The FORD Sunday Evening Hour . . . ABC, Sundays, 8-9 p.m., E.D.S.T.

1946 MERCURY

More OF EVERYTHING YOU WANT WITH Mercury

For more real fun, here's the car for you—the spirited Mercury Station Wagon. You'll like its country club styling . . . and its practicality too! Here is the answer to all your motoring needs. More capacity . . . it carries eight in comfort! More usefulness . . . it does utility hauling! More beauty . . . its youthful smartness is equally at home in town or country! Drive it, and see why Mercury gives you more of everything!

MERCURY—DIVISION OF FORD MOTOR COMPANY

MORE ROOM Look inside! Ample room for eight, with space to spare! Those comfortable seats are genuine leather, skillfully tailored in a choice of colors: tan, red or gray. It's a big, handsome car, for big families with lots of friends!

MORE STYLE Superb design and coachwork give the Mercury Station Wagon a smart, custom-built look. Maple body framing is combined with birch or deep-toned mahogany panels, for extra richness. A stand-out, wherever it goes!

MORE CONVENIENCE By far, the most useful type of car on the road! Center, rear seats are removable to triple storage space. Sloping tail-gate lowers for easy loading and added length. Here's all the room you need, and more!

TUNE IN . . . THE FORD-Bob Crosby Show—CBS, WEDNESDAYS, 9.30-10 P.M., E.S.T. . . . THE FORD SUNDAY EVENING HOUR—ABC, SUNDAYS, 8-9 P.M., E.S.T.

1946 MERCURY

Away Out Ahead — Automatically!

Series "66" Club Sedan, popular model of Oldsmobile's lowest-priced line.

with

Proved in seven years of owner service . . . still the *newest* thing in driving!

Optional at extra cost.

One touch of your toe and you glide out ahead . . . smoothly, *automatically* . . . in the brilliant new Oldsmobile with GM Hydra-Matic Drive.* Stoplight to stoplight, city to city, you *never* shift gears, you *never* touch a clutch. There's not even a clutch pedal in the car. You step on the gas . . . you steer . . . you step on the brake; Hydra-Matic Drive does all the rest . . . *automatically!*

And the new Oldsmobile is just as easy on the eyes as it is in the driving! Its smooth, tailored styling and tastefully appointed interiors are already setting the pace for next year's cars—winning attention . . . winning admiration . . . *automatically!*

Listen to Henry J. Taylor, on the air for GM twice weekly. See newspaper for time and station.

Oldsmobile

A GENERAL MOTORS QUALITY CAR

1946 Oldsmobile Series "66" Club Sedan

"Riding Habit"
THAT'S TRULY SMART !

The *Oldsmobile habit* is always in style . . . with America's smartest people. They like the flowing smoothness of Oldsmobile's lines . . . modern . . . streamlined . . . in perfect good taste. They enjoy the gliding comfort of Oldsmobile's ride . . . cradled on Quadri-Coil Springs . . . steadied by 4-Way Stabilization. They respect Oldsmobile's reputation as a "thoroughbred" . . . the latest and greatest product of America's oldest motor car manufacturer.

Forward-looking people particularly appreciate Oldsmobile's engineering leadership . . . so well exemplified in GM Hydra-Matic Drive. Gears shift automatically through all four forward speeds. There's no clutch pedal in the car. Driving becomes amazingly simple . . . all you do is step on the gas and steer.

It's *smart* to ride in an Oldsmobile . . . *smart* to drive one . . . especially if it's a *new* Oldsmobile with General Motors' *new and finer* Hydra-Matic Drive. (Optional at extra cost on all new models.)

KEEP AMERICA'S HIGHWAYS SAFE—DRIVE CAREFULLY

"Driving Habit"
YOU'RE SURE TO LIKE, TOO !

Oldsmobile

A GENERAL MOTORS VALUE

1946 Oldsmobile

FINEST OF THE FAMOUS
"Silver Streaks"

This is the new Pontiac—a car that adds new luster to a fine old name. It carries to an even higher level the tradition of quality that began when the first Pontiac "Silver Streak" was introduced a decade ago. If you are a Pontiac owner you know what that statement means— because four years of wartime driving have proved that Pontiac quality pays great dividends in owner satisfaction. And if you have never owned a Pontiac, we believe you will be greatly impressed by this fine new car. In appearance, in all-around performance, in comfort—*in everything that stands for quality*— it is the finest of the famous "Silver Streaks."

NEW PONTIAC

PONTIAC MOTOR DIVISION • GENERAL MOTORS CORPORATION

1946 Pontiac Silver Streak

People are saying —

"You *get* more – *save* more – when you buy Chevrolet!"

Yes, you get more beauty, comfort and all-round performance with economy in this new Chevrolet than in any other car in its field . . . and you also save money on purchase price, operation and upkeep . . . for Chevrolet alone gives **BIG-CAR QUALITY AT LOWEST COST!**

Whenever and wherever people talk motor cars—and almost everybody's doing it these days—you'll find the tide of favor running more and more strongly toward this *bigger-looking, better-looking* new Chevrolet for 1947.

That is true because men and women are convinced that this car gives *BIG-CAR QUALITY AT LOWEST COST*—takes extra-good care of their desires as well as their dollars . . . and your own tests will tell you they're right.

CHEVROLET MOTOR DIVISION, *GENERAL MOTORS CORPORATION*, DETROIT 2, MICHIGAN

Look at the new Chevrolet and you'll see it's the only car in its field with the luxurious *Big-Car beauty* of a Body by Fisher. Drive it and you'll know it's the only car in its field giving the *Big-Car performance and dependability* of the famous Valve-in-Head Thrift-Master Engine. Ride in it and you'll realize it's the only car in its field combining the *Big-Car comfort and safety* of the Unitized Knee-Action Ride and Positive-Action Hydraulic Brakes.

And yet this beautifully balanced line of Chevrolet motor cars is the *lowest-priced* line in its field, and owners will tell you it has the lowest operating and upkeep costs as well!

You get more, and you save more, when you buy Chevrolet . . . the only car giving *BIG-CAR QUALITY AT LOWEST COST* . . . and the wisest investment for you.

People are saying,

"You'll prefer Chevrolet... Smartest buy of '47!"

1947 CHEVROLET

1947 CHEVROLET

ople are saying—

"It's the *smoothest-riding* car we've ever owned!"

Purr... How can there be such surging power, such exciting acceleration in an engine that purrs so softly? Simply this . . . no other engine parts in any car are finished to the degree of smoothness Chrysler achieves with its exclusive Superfinish. Pioneered by Chrysler engineers, Superfinish is typical of the great advances that make it more fun, more satisfying to own a beautiful Chrysler.

the Beautiful Chrysler

WITH HYDRAULICALLY OPERATED TRANSMISSION AND gyrol FLUID DRIVE

1947 CHEVROLET STATION WAGON

1947 CHRYSLER

1947 Dodge

1947 Dodge

1947 Ford

Ford's out Front

WITH A FAMILY AFFAIR!

Do you know why more people have picked Ford station wagons than any other make? Here's one reason: Ford pioneered the station wagon . . . introduced this smart utility model to an appreciative public. Yes, Ford has produced more cars of this body type than all other makers put together.

Today Ford Continues to build its own station wagon bodies at Iron Mountain, Michigan . . . selects the finest native hardwoods for them . . . fashions them with real cabinetmaker craftsmanship. "It's the best looking, longest lasting station wagon on the road today," say owners . . . "Way out front in popularity!"

There's a *Ford* in your future

AS A ROOMY 8-PASSENGER CAR

AS A FAMILY UTILITY CARRY-ALL

Really two cars in one! Eight people can travel comfortably in the Ford station wagon . . . and in real style! And for light hauling, both rear seats are easily, quickly removable. It's the handiest carry-all ever . . . a real family affair!

1947 FORD

1947 CHEVROLET

1947 HUDSONS

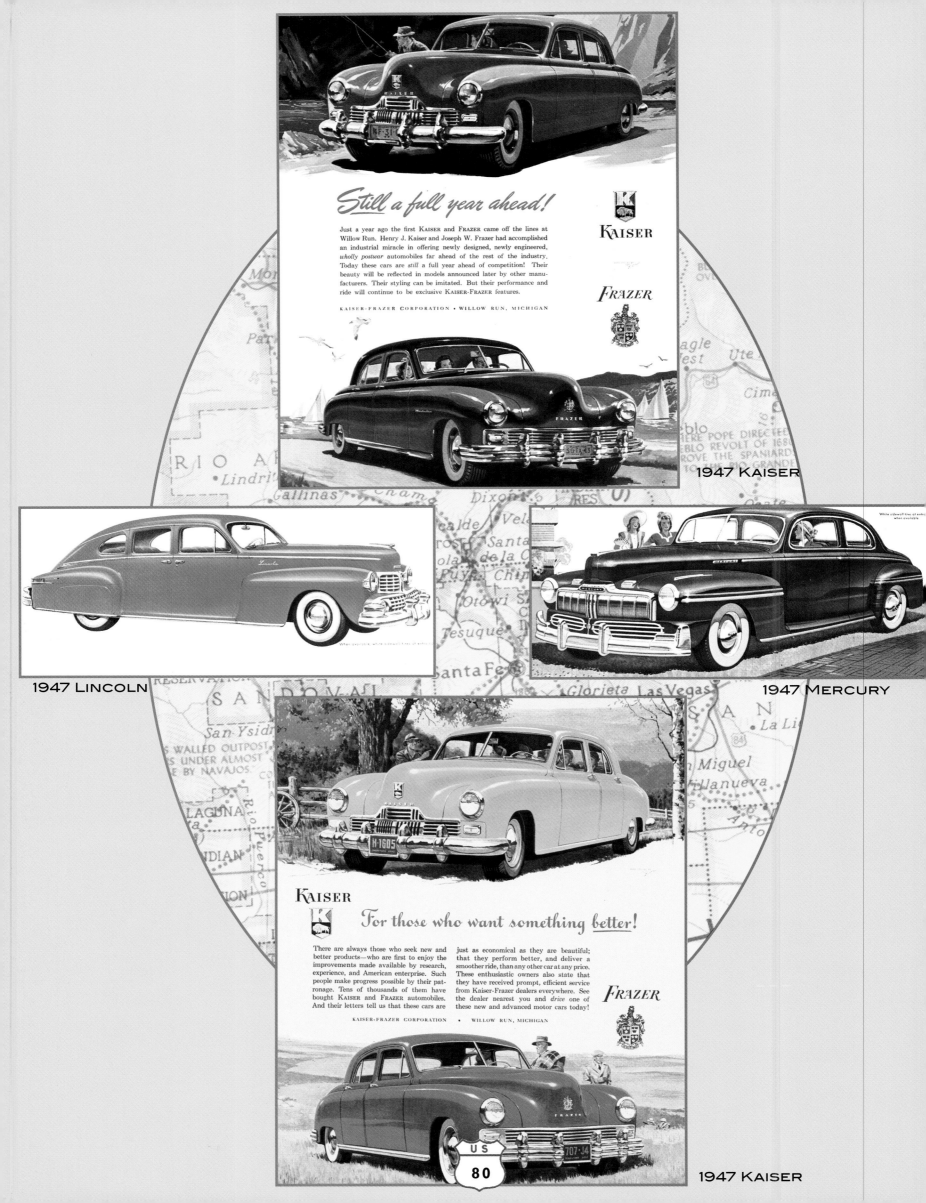

Still a full year ahead!

Just a year ago the first KAISER and FRAZER came off the lines at Willow Run. Henry J. Kaiser and Joseph W. Frazer had accomplished an industrial miracle in offering newly designed, newly engineered, *wholly postwar* automobiles far ahead of the rest of the industry. Today these cars are *still* a full year ahead of competition! Their beauty will be reflected in models announced later by other manufacturers. Their styling can be imitated. But their performance and ride will continue to be exclusive KAISER-FRAZER features.

KAISER-FRAZER CORPORATION • WILLOW RUN, MICHIGAN

KAISER

FRAZER

1947 KAISER

1947 LINCOLN

1947 MERCURY

For those who want something better!

KAISER

There are always those who seek new and better products—who are first to enjoy the improvements made available by research, experience, and American enterprise. Such people make progress possible by their patronage. Tens of thousands of them have bought KAISER and FRAZER automobiles. And their letters tell us that these cars are just as economical as they are beautiful; that they perform better, and deliver a smoother ride, than any other car at any price. These enthusiastic owners also state that they have received prompt, efficient service from Kaiser-Frazer dealers everywhere. See the dealer nearest you and *drive* one of these new and advanced motor cars today!

KAISER-FRAZER CORPORATION • WILLOW RUN, MICHIGAN

FRAZER

1947 KAISER

MORE OF EVERYTHING YOU WANT
WITH THE 1947 *Mercury*

1947 MERCURY

It's *Smart*
to own
an Olds

It's *Smart* to go automatic . . .

Takes more than a spring shower to dim the beauty of this big new 1947 Oldsmobile. It's smart in appearance . . . it's smooth in performance . . . come rain or shine. Fact is, when wet weather slows down the traffic, that's when you really appreciate driving without shifting gears or pushing a clutch—the Hydra-Matic way. It's safer, too, because GM Hydra-Matic Drive* gives smoother power under perfect control — *automatically!* No wonder so many *smart* people choose Oldsmobile this year!

(White sidewall tires at extra cost when available.)

The coat—a new All-Weather Topper by Duchess Royal. The car—a new "98" 4-Door Sedan by Oldsmobile.

Oldsmobile

OFFERING

GM GENERAL MOTORS **HYDRA-MATIC DRIVE**

*Optional at extra cost.

1947 OLDSMOBILE

It's *Smart*
to own
an Olds

Oldsmobile

WITH GM GENERAL MOTORS **HYDRA-MATIC DRIVE**

*Optional at extra cost.

Swim suit designed by Tina Leser
Convertible Coupe by Oldsmobile.

1947 OLDSMOBILE CONVERTIBLE COUPE

1947 Mercury

1947 Plymouth

A fine car made finer

PONTIAC

Be happy
with your next car!

It is a great satisfaction to own a car that you *really like* —
one that you can look forward to driving, each day, with
pleasurable anticipation. Pontiac owners say this is one
of the great extra values that come with a Pontiac car.
Regardless of the year it is built, a Pontiac gives *outstanding* performance — compared with other cars in its
field. We sincerely believe this is something you ought to
consider — whether you expect to get your new car this
year, next year, or *any year*. You'd be *happy* with a Pontiac!

For 1947, Pontiac offers 10 beautiful body types,
in two series, Torpedoes and Streamliners. Included in the line are the stunning cars shown
above — the Streamliner Sedan Coupe, the Streamliner Station Wagon and the Torpedo Convertible.

PONTIAC MOTOR DIVISION of GENERAL MOTORS CORPORATION

1947 PONTIAC STREAMLINER SEDAN-
COUPE, STREAMLINER STATION
WAGON, TORPEDO CONVERTIBLE

Presenting the new

1947 PONTIAC
SILVER STREAKS

1947 PONTIAC SILVER STREAK

*Ever drive across
this famous bridge?*

1948 CHEVROLET

*Only One
is Number One!*

Only
CHEVROLET
IS FIRST!

America's biggest
money's worth!

Keep your eye on this fact when you choose
your next car: More people buy Chevrolets
than any other make because Chevrolet gives them more value;
and this is true this year as for the total 17-year period, 1931 to
date! Yes, only one is Number One, only Chevrolet is first, because
only Chevrolet gives BIG-CAR QUALITY AT LOWEST COST.

CHEVROLET MOTOR DIVISION, GENERAL MOTORS CORPORATION, DETROIT 2, MICHIGAN

1948 CHEVROLET

1948 DODGE

1948 DODGE

PEOPLE'S CHOICE

Seems as though nearly everybody wants Dodge All-Fluid Drive!

Dodge All-Fluid Drive takes the fight out of stop-and-go traffic driving . . . gives starts and stop...

features . . . extra-roomy interiors . . . full-width "Chair-Height" seats . . . leg room...

VOTING BOOTH

Ford's out Front down on the Farm

V-8 or Six, there's horsepower to spare in the Ford.

No matter how much moola you lay o... the line. Ford is the only car to offe... you a choice of a V-8 or a Six!

Wool, and lots of it, goes into Ford upholstery. No wonder it wears so well and looks so beautiful.

You can run a Ford almost for chicken feed, thanks to 4-ring aluminum pistons and balanced carburetion. Ford economy is something to crow about!

There's nothing stubborn about the way Ford starts. Just touch a button and you take off!

There's a Ford in your future

No use Mac. You can't beat a Ford!

A cat can look at a queen and that's what the Ford car is — a 'queen' inside and out.

1948 FORD

Ford's out Front in Allen's Alley

Fred Allen and his Gang tell why:

"MAMA'S WRITING A NEW NATIONAL ANTHEM ABOUT FORD VISIBILITY—'OH BOY, CAN YOU SEE!'"

"PORTLAND, AS THE RECORD SAID TO THE DISC JOCKEY, 'LET'S TAKE A SPIN!'"

"FORD'S MAH PERENNIAL CANDIDATE, SON. MAH NEW CAMPAIGN SLOGAN IS,' WATCH FORD IN '48'...'48, THAT IS!"

SEN. CLAGHORN

MRS. NUSSBAUM

"MINE HUSBAND, PIERRE, SAYS THAT WHEN HE'S RIDING IN A FORD CAR HE'S COZY AS A HERRING IN SOUR CREAM."

AJAX CASSIDY

"A FORD COSTS LESS TO FEED THAN A COW IN CLOVER, BUB."

"ME BOY, THAT BAKED-ON FINISH IS SHINIER THAN THE BRASS RAIL AT KERRIGAN'S KOZY KORNER."

TITUS MOODY

"V-8 OR SIX, FOR... HUMS A PRETTY DI...

THE DEMARCO SISTERS

...NE IN...THE FRED ALLEN SHOW— ...C. SUNDAYS, 8:30 PM, E.S.T.

There's a Ford in your futu...

1948 FORD

US 84

1948 FORD

Eight body styles in the Super Series and Commodore Custom Series. Your choice, 121 h.p. all-new Super-Six or 128 h.p. improved Super-Eight engine. New type Super-Cushion tires. Ten rich body colors. Two special colors or five two-tone combinations—white sidewall tires—at slight extra cost.

1948 Hudson

1948 Hudson
Commodore
Custom Sedan

"This time it's Hudson!"

Why not get all this in your new car?
Owners of low-built Hudsons have it!

Designers have known it for a long time, and now owners of New Hudsons—the lowest cars on the highway—are seeing for themselves that the lower a car can be built, the more graceful its lines can be made, the better it will perform and ride, the more surely it will handle, and the safer it will be!

Your own family photograph album will show you that the trend to the low-built automobile has been going on for years. In fact, no manufacturer has ever introduced a new model that was higher than its predecessor!

But something else has been going on, too! Whenever designers have attempted the ideal in low-built cars *without lowering interior floors*, they've had to keep top lines high to preserve inside head room, or reduce roominess to get top lines down—and thus they've compromised and fallen short of their real purpose.

The New Hudson changes all this!

This remarkable motor car has *recessed floors* that permit lounge-size seats to be moved down to harmonize with the new, lower top. Because Hudson owners "step down", they have more head room—in a car that is only five feet from ground to top—than in any automobile now in volume production—and all this with ample road clearance!

But roominess is only a small fraction of the wonderful things you get with the modern design for '49.* Cast your eyes about this page—see what can be yours when you own the car that is so far ahead *—it* is a *protected investment* in motor-car value! Hudso. Motor Car Company, Detroit 14.

Only Hudson Brings You All These PLUS FEATURES!

Automatic gear shifting in forward speeds with Hudson Drive-Master Transmission—shifts only when you want, but does all the work . . . Your choice, **Super-Six** or **Super-Eight** engine—the most powerful American Six built today, and a masterful Eight . . . **Triple-Safe Brakes**—lines hydraulic system with reserve mechanical system on same pedal, plus finger tip release parking brake . . . **Weather-Control**—Hudson's heater-conditioned-air system . . . **Super-Cushion Tires** . . . **Center-Point Steering** . . . and more than 20 other important features on display at the nearest Hudson dealer's.

*The many advantages of Hudson's "Step-Down" design are fully explained and illustrated in a booklet available at all Hudson dealers.

†Optional at slight extra cost.

Hudson has authentic, low-built beauty, acclaimed from road to road, because the "step-down" principle is so basically right it frees designers of the need for makeshift styling, enables Hudson to achieve pleasing proportions and symmetry, free-flowing lines.

Here's a heaping portion of roominess and comfort—more head room and the roomiest seats in any mass-produced car built today, because you "step down", and because seats are ahead of the rear wheels and extend the full width of the body.

Hudson gives you a hug-the-road ride, especially on curves, and a smooth, steady way of going that is "out of this world", because it has the lowest center of gravity in any American stock car!

The lowest-built car on the highway, yet Hudson has amazing head room and ample road clearance

The only car you step down into
NEW Hudson

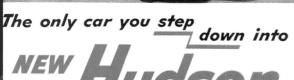

Hudson floors are recessed down within the frame (shown in red, upper above), seats are lowered, so you get more than ample head room in the only car with the new, lower silhouette.

You ride down within a base frame (shown in red, lower above), and rear seats are positioned ahead of the rear wheels so that full body width is available for wonderfully roomy seats—four inches wider than the car itself.

A wholly new measure of safety, because of Hudson's new Mono-bilt body-and-frame* which completely encircles you, even outside the rear wheels, with sturdy, box-section steel girders. There's added safety, too, in Hudson's steadiness, and in the smooth, sure way in which this car handles on the road.

*Trade-mark and patents pending.

Performance? You bet! Hudson offers you an all-new, high-compression, 121 h.p. Super-Six—most powerful American-built Six—or a masterful 128 h.p. Super-Eight. Both get every chance to perform at their brilliant best, because this car is the lowest built, most stream-lined of them all!

Eight body styles in Super Series and Commodore Custom Series. Ten rich body colors. Two special colors or five two-tone combinations—white sidewall tires—at extra cost.

1948 Hudson

MOST FOR YOUR MONEY

One sure way to protect your motor car investment is to buy a KAISER or a FRAZER. For in either of these ultra-modern cars you buy *lasting value.* You buy styling that will still be out ahead when many of today's so-called "new" cars have been obsoleted by their own manufacturers!

And at the same time you buy *fully postwar engineering!* A new power-to-weight ratio and truly advanced chassis design give results that will mean "money in the bank" for you in years to come. How can you possibly get more for your transportation money than to buy a car that in itself offers insurance against high and quick obsolescence?

KAISER-FRAZER CORPORATION • WILLOW RUN, MICHIGAN

1948 KAISER-FRAZER

What's new that's <u>not</u> from Willow Run?

As more and more manufacturers get around to announcing *their* post-war models, the compelling influence of Kaiser-Frazer styling becomes increasingly apparent. The *beauty* of the KAISER and the FRAZER has been paid the ultimate compliment—attempted imitation!

And K-F *engineering* has also defied duplication. Phenomenal performance with such unexpected economy is still unique. K-F chassis construction provides a new distribution of mass and load, cradles *both* seats between the axles—gives a "gliding ride" no other car has equalled! K-F's combination of roominess, roadability and ease of control is still supreme! Your dealer can *demonstrate* other *exclusives.*

KAISER-FRAZER CORPORATION • WILLOW RUN, MICHIGAN

Hear *Newscope* with
Wendell Noble, 4 times weekly
over Mutual

1948 KAISER-FRAZER

1948 MERCURY

More OF EVERYTHING YOU WANT
WITH *Mercury*

1948 OLDSMOBILE

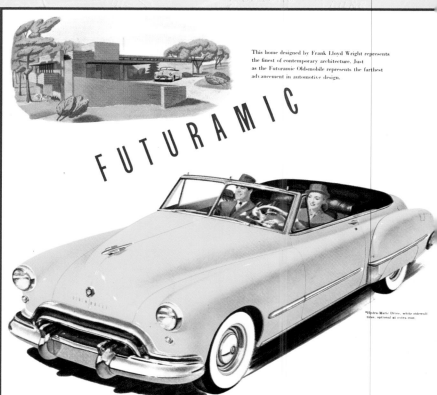

This home designed by Frank Lloyd Wright represents the finest of contemporary architecture. Just as the Futuramic Oldsmobile represents the farthest advancement in automotive design.

FUTURAMIC

*Hydra-Matic Drive, white sidewall
tires, optional at extra cost.*

FUTURAMIC

Architect George Fred Keck built
tomorrow's way of living into this new home
...just as tomorrow's *way of driving* is
built into the Futuramic Oldsmobile!

Look fast...you'll catch a glimpse of tomorrow...it's a Futuramic Oldsmobile swinging into action! Watch it as it wings down the road
...the sleek, low lines blending with the breeze...that massive hood ahead of the pack. Then slip behind the wheel of the Futuramic
Oldsmobile and let GM Hydra-Matic Drive* take over! You'll ride a high tide of power out into the clear...without ever touching a
clutch or shift! And to climb a hill...pass another car...or whisk out of danger...just step on the accelerator and *Whirlaway!*
Once you've known this "thrill of tomorrow," you'll also know why the Futuramic Oldsmobile is making new highway history!

FUTURAMIC **OLDSMOBILE**

1948 OLDSMOBILE

Designed by the Wizards of "Ah's!"

WATCH the envious glances—hear the enthusiastic "Oh's!" and "Ah's!"—when this sleek, glossy Packard convertible glides up to the curb!

For here is a gloriously new and daring concept of what a convertible should really be—and every breath-taking inch of it is Packard precision-built.

Its husky, newly-engineered chassis (*100 pounds heavier than that of the sedan*) gives this convertible a safety, a rigidity, an in-the-slot stability and quietness no other

Packard convertible has ever matched.

The new straight-eight Packard engine—whether it's the 145-h.p. Super or the 160-h.p. Custom—gives you a brilliance of performance and a whispering surge of reserve power such as you've never known.

In its rich interior appointments there's dazzling beauty, and a touch of magic, too. Press a button and the top lowers or raises. Another button moves the front seat forward or backward! And *all four* windows have magic push-button control!

Don't deny yourself the thrill of seeing the glamor car of '48 at your Packard dealer's!

ASK THE MAN WHO OWNS ONE

THE NEW
PACKARD

Out of this world...
into your ♥ heart!

The Packard Station Sedan is an entirely *new kind* of car. Here's sedan luxury for six—with the easy-loading, carryall utility of a station wagon. All steel, finished in Northern Birch.

1948 PACKARD

1948 PLYMOUTH

1949 BUICK

Looks fine for '49

of Fireball Power!

No clutch pedal! It's got Dynaflow Drive!

Look at all the room!

The lines are lovely!

This Roomy 4-Door Sedan seats six, has 22% more glass area. On ROADMASTER or SUPER chassis. White sidewall tires, as illustrated, available at extra cost.

87

CHEVROLET

First for Quality at Lowest Cost

1949 CHEVROLET STYLELINE
DE LUXE FOUR-DOOR SEDAN

OVER ALL...
all over America!

The Styleline De Luxe 4-Door Sedan
White sidewall tires optional at extra cost.

Yes, in city after city, town
after town and state after
state—in all parts of America
—there are more Chevrolets
in use than any other make!

The most Beautiful **BUY** *of all!*

1949 CHEVROLET STYLELINE DE
LUXE FOUR-DOOR SEDAN

THRILL *With Young America*

CHOOSE THIS LOWER PRICED
NEW DODGE *WAYFARER*

Dodge gives you the first new Sports Roadster . . . a new
value-packed 2-door Sedan . . . a new 3-passenger Coupe . . .
for just a few dollars more than the lowest priced cars.

You'll have to see it to believe it!
Even then, you'll wonder how the
exciting new Dodge Wayfarer can be
priced so low.

You'll see how Dodge "functional
styling" gives new basic beauty . . .
new roominess *inside* with less bulk
outside!

You'll be amazed at Dodge Wayfarer
performance, too. In traffic, you'll find
the Wayfarer just as eager and just as

nimble as a polo pony—because of its
115" wheelbase and more powerful
"Get-Away" Engine. And there's the
thrilling smoothness of Dodge gyrol
Fluid Drive . . . smoother starts and
stops . . . smoother driving mile after
mile.

See the new, *lower-priced* Wayfarer
. . . every inch a rugged, dependable
Dodge. One look . . . one ride will
tell you here is the car that gives
more for your money today.

ONLY CAR OF ITS KIND! The smart good looks
of a convertible without the high price tag.

The New Lower Priced **DODGE**
WAYFARER
With gyrol FLUID DRIVE

1949 DODGE WAYFARER

1949 FORD

1949 FORD

1949 FRAZER MANHATTAN

1949 FORD

1949 HUDSON CUSTOM COMMODORE SEDAN

Alert buyers are following the signs to the

New Hudson
America's "4-Most" car !

1949 HUDSON

1949 HUDSON COMMODORE CLUB COUPE

1949 LINCOLN COSMOPOLITAN
CONVERTIBLE

1949 LINCOLN COSMOPOLITAN
SPORT SEDAN

1949 LINCOLN

"Custom"
Comfort!
...that's the Lincoln Idea

The "custom" touch adds more luxury, more elegance, to the 1949 Lincoln Cosmopolitan!

Naturally, you expect to enjoy comfort and luxury in a fine automobile.

But the special luxurious comfort of the 1949 Lincoln Cosmopolitan will exceed your expectations!

No other fine car offers you a wider "custom" choice of rich upholstery and trim...or such elegant interior refinements. (Even electrically operated windows are "standard" on this car!)

And the interior is more spacious than ever, with broad seats, foam-rubber cushions and ample leg room for truly restful motoring.

Visibility, too, is on the same generous scale. The Lincoln Cosmopolitan windshield is a glistening one-piece arc of safety glass almost five feet wide. What an aid to your vision as you drive!

And never have you driven such a thoroughly comfortable car. It rides as smoothly as a drifting cloud...handles lightly. Its engine—the great new Lincoln V-type "Eight"—has no equal for all-round durability, low operating cost and efficiency. Its powerful new brakes are unsurpassed for safe, gentle stops...another comfort to your peace of mind!

Nothing—simply nothing—has been spared to make this Lincoln Cosmopolitan the most luxurious, comfortable car of all. Ask your dealer for a demonstration ride tomorrow—and discover this yourself.

LINCOLN-MERCURY DIVISION OF FORD MOTOR COMPANY

White side-wall tires, rear lamps (and rear wheel shields on the Lincoln) are optional at extra cost.

1949 LINCOLN COSMOPOLITAN

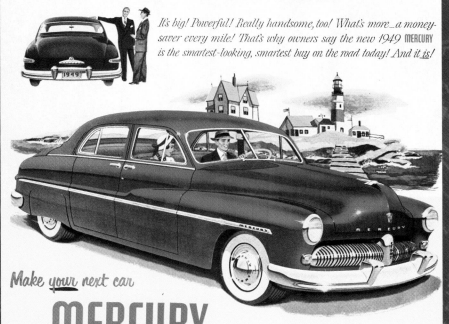

"It's smarter to own a MERCURY!"

THAT'S WHAT OWNERS SAY ABOUT THIS HANDSOME NEW 1949 CAR!

It's big! Powerful! Really handsome, too! What's more...a money-saver every mile! That's why owners say the new 1949 MERCURY is the smartest-looking, smartest buy on the road today! And it is!

Make your next car

MERCURY

YOU'LL find it's smarter to own a Mercury, too! For everything in it has been *road-proven* by thousands of owners for millions of miles!

You get a new 8-cylinder, V-type engine with surprising *economy*. Front coil *springing!* A truly restful "com-fort-zone" *ride!* Easier *steering!* "Super-safety" *brakes!* Increased all-round *visibility!* Plus the luxury of foam rubber-cushioned *seats!*

See it! Drive it—and you'll say: "It's Mercury for me!"

MERCURY DIVISION OF FORD MOTOR COMPANY

White side-wall tires and rear wheel shields optional at extra cost

1949 MERCURY

"Thrifty? You bet it is!"

THAT'S WHAT OWNERS SAY ABOUT THE POWERFUL NEW 1949 MERCURY ENGINE!

Imagine getting 17...18...19* miles per gallon and up! Owners say this long, low, road-proven MERCURY does it every day! They claim it's the thriftiest, most-practical-to-own-car they've ever driven! And it is!

*and even more with optional Overdrive

Make your next car MERCURY

IN your 1949 Mercury, *economy* isn't merely a promise. It's a *fact*—already *proven* in millions of miles of daily driving!

And everything else about your new, road-hugging 1949 Mercury is tried and *proven*, too.

You get a new 8-cylinder, V-type en-gine with terrific *power!* Front coil *springing!* A truly restful "comfort-zone" *ride!* Easier *steering!* "Super-safety" *brakes!* Softer, broader *seating!* Increased *visibility!*

So, come in and see it. You'll say "It's Mercury for me!"

LINCOLN-MERCURY DIVISION OF FORD MOTOR COMPANY

White side-wall tires and rear wheel shields are optional

1949 MERCURY

NEW "Holiday" COUPÉ

1949 OLDSMOBILE HOLIDAY COUPE

White sidewall tires, chrome wheel covers, scuff guards and radio optional at extra co...

1949 PLYMOUTH

the car that likes to be compared

Inside and out... **PLYMOUTH** BUILDS GREAT CARS

The instant you step through the wide-opening doors of the new Plymouth, you are taken with the interior roominess and richness of appointments. You relax in chair-height seats that are wider and deeper from front to back. There's room for long legs *and* high hats.

The new instrument panel, with its richly grained finish, groups gauges for easy reading. By simply turning a key, you turn on the ignition, start the engine, put the automatic choke in operation—all at once! Greatly enlarged windshield and rear window give better visibility. Whether you choose pile fabric or rich broadcloth, you get smart, long-wearing upholstery materials that harmonize with body colors. The luxury of the entire ensemble is highlighted with gleaming chrome and plastic.

But it's not just on its face value that the new Plymouth likes to be compared. Drive this great car and discover for yourself its greater power and safety, its luxurious riding comfort, its amazing ease of handling. Compare—and let the ride decide!

PLYMOUTH Division of CHRYSLER CORPORATION, Detroit 31, Michigan

Luxurious interior of the beautiful Plymouth Special De Luxe 4-Door Sedan. Insert is the newly designed instrument panel.

White sidewall tires, chrome wheel covers and rear fender scuff guards optional at extra cost.

1949 PLYMOUTH SPECIAL DE LUXE FOUR-DOOR SEDAN

1949 PLYMOUTH

PONTIAC

because it brings you luxury...

at its lowest cost

1949 PONTIAC

1950 BUICK ROADMASTER

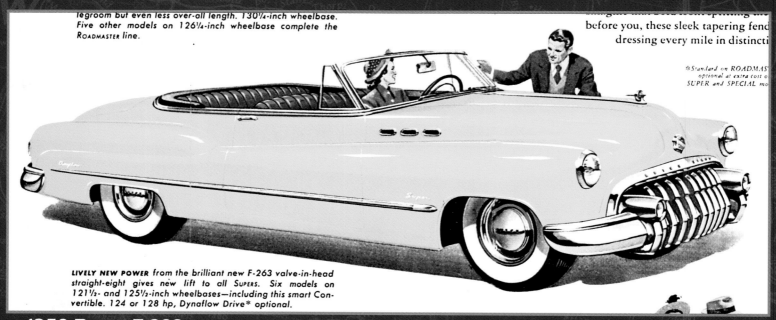

legroom but even less over-all length. 130¼-inch wheelbase. Five other models on 126¼-inch wheelbase complete the ROADMASTER line.

before you, these sleek tapering fend... dressing every mile in distincti...

*Standard on ROADMAS... optional at extra cost o... SUPER and SPECIAL mo...

LIVELY NEW POWER from the brilliant new F-263 valve-in-head straight-eight gives new lift to all SUPERS. Six models on 121½- and 125½-inch wheelbases—including this smart Convertible. 124 or 128 hp, Dynaflow Drive* optional.

1950 BUICK F-263

1950 BUICK

1950 Chevrolet

1950 Chevrolet
Styleline De Luxe
Four-Door Sedan

1950 Chevrolet

1950 Chevrolet

1950 Chrysler Crown Imperial Limousine

1950 Ford Fordor Sedan, Convertible

1950 Ford Station Wagon, Custom Deluxe Tudor

1950 FORD

1950 FORD

1950 FORD

1950 HUDSON CUSTOM
COMMODORE SERIES
FOUR-DOOR SEDAN

1950 HUDSON

1950 LINCOLN

HAVE YOU DRIVEN THE NEW *Lincolns?*

PRESENTING THE NEW *Lincolns*

1950 LINCOLN COSMOPOLITANS

1950 MERCURYS

1950 OLDSMOBILES

Shiftless....and very proud of it!

New 150-HP SUPER DELUXE Touring Sedan

1950 PACKARD EIGHT

There's never been anything like

Packard Ultramatic Drive

You'll have no clutch pedal to push . . . no gears to shift. And those are just the *first* two points to remember about Packard Ultramatic Drive!

You'll never be annoyed by jerking or clunking, or "racing engine sensation". . . never bothered by gas-wasting slippage at cruising speeds . . . never "out-smarted" by complicated automatic controls.

In *every* phase of motoring, Packard Ultramatic Drive brings you wonderful new driving ease . . . be-

cause it begins with new basic *principles*.

Born of a 16-year Packard development program—backed by $7,000,000 in new manufacturing facilities —Packard Ultramatic Drive is now available, at extra cost, on an increasing number of models.

Don't miss a demonstration of this amazing new drive! Once you've heard the whole exciting story, you'll know why impartial technical observers call it "the *last word* in automatic, no-shift control!"

A S K   T H E   M A N   W H O   O W N S   O N E

More responsive: No slippage at cruising speeds. No lag, waiting for gears to shift. For instant bursts of acceleration—just "*tramp down!*"

More positive: No over-heating of the drive mechanism during long climbs. Smooth, gradual engine braking on down-grades.

More flexible: Choice of *acceleration* or *cruising*, in both low and high range! Easy change from Forward to Reverse without clashing

1950 PACKARD EIGHT

A WONDERFUL CAR TO OWN—A WONDERFUL CAR TO DRI
A WONDERFUL CAR TO BE SEEN IN!
AND PRICED JUST ABOVE THE VERY LOWEST!

1950 PONTIAC

Plymouth Packed with value and ready to prove it

P.S. The 48 states are packed with lots of other things, too, but there isn't room (or rhyme) to fit them in. But there *is* room to tell you that Plymouth is packed with value. The convenience of Ignition Key Starting . . . the positive protection of Safety-Rim Wheels . . . the comfort of Air Pillow Ride . . . these are just a small sample of what this great car offers you. See your nearby Plymouth dealer now. He'll be glad to arrange a demonstration drive.

PLYMOUTH Division of CHRYSLER CORPORATION, Detroit 31, Michigan

PLYMOUTH
BUILDS GREAT CARS

1950 PLYMOUTH

1950 PONTIAC Catalina

PONTIAC
Catalina

Now on Display!

AT YOUR PONTIAC DEALER

Distinctive BEAUTY . . Magnificent PERFORMANCE . . Long Range ECONOMY

ALL ARE YOURS IN A PONTIAC AT VERY LOW COST

1950 PONTIAC

FIREBALL POWERED

All-Star Line-up for '51

Your first eye-smacking look at the line of lovelies pictured here tells you that they've got what it takes in visual charm.

But the fellow who said a picture speaks louder than a thousand words wasn't talking about these superbly able 1951 Buicks.

Sure, they're smart to look at—smart in style and smart in dress.

But they're also smartly powered—smartly engineered—smartly priced. And it would take a book to describe in full their deep-down goodness.

What's been done for '51 is to take the best automobiles that ever bore the Buick name—and top them.

Come, look them over, and you'll see what we mean.

There's the SPECIAL which can accurately be titled "the newest car in the world"—new in structure, new in power, new in dimensions, new in thrift—and potent in price appeal.

There's the CUSTOM SPECIAL that brings new luxury to the low-price field.

There's the SUPER—that looks and is a smart new edition of its "best seller" forebear.

Then there's the ROADMASTER—that coddles your anatomy on luxurious new fabrics and cloud-soft cushions—pampers your pride with its lordly bearing—shoots a delicious tingle right up your spine by the exuberance of its power and action.

We could go on and on. This is the car that "breathes through its nose." This is the car that sports a brand-new front-end styling. This is the car with new high-visibility instrument dials, more easily read at night. This is the car with glare-and-heat-reducing glass* and a host of other news-making features you can't afford to miss.

So your No. 1 date this week end is with your Buick dealer. It won't take you long to conclude that he's offering the smartest buys of the year.

*Optional at extra cost on all models. (Not presently available.)

"Smart Buy's Buick"

See them first tomorrow...

1951 BUICK

1951 CHEVROLET BEL AIR

CHEVROLET
Best Buy on the Road!

A Smart Customer!

You bet! Anyone is smart to drive a new Chevrolet. Why? Well, look. Have you ever seen a better looking car? And take it from me. It drives better, rides better, *is* better. Costs less to own, too!

Room? Just Look!

No space problem here! There's room aplenty — room for luggage, groceries, almost anything. That pop-up trunk lid is swell, too!

Wish I had Powerglide!*

There's nothin' like it! No clutch pedal. No gearshifting. Just touch the accelerator and go. *Really smooth,* too! For *my* money, Powerglide beats everything else on the road.

Such a Comfortable Car!

It's wonderful! So easy to drive. So comfortable to ride in. Seems like you just float along the highway!

Yes, Sir! That's my Choice!

Wouldn't drive anything else! And if you take *my* advice, mister, you'll head for your Chevrolet dealer's *right now!*

*Combination of Powerglide automatic transmission and 105-h.p. engine optional in De Luxe models at extra cost. Model illustrated is style line De Luxe 4-door sedan. (Continuation of standard equipment and trim illustrated is dependent on availability of material.) CHEVROLET DIVISION OF GENERAL MOTORS, DETROIT 2, MICHIGAN.

CHEVROLET

The Smart New Styleline De Luxe 4-Door Sedan

You'll like its longer, lower, wider BIG-CAR LOOK!

CHEVROLET

1951 CHEVROLET Styleline De Luxe Four-Door Sedan

SPECIAL TODAY

Compare FORD with America's Highest Priced Cars
You can pay more but you can't buy better!

"I'd rather take the Ford"

1951 CHRYSLER

1951 FORD

CHEVROLET

American as cider in the fall,
Reliable as the good earth,
Familiar as a roadside stand,
That's Chevrolet—America's favorite car!

1951 CHEVROLET

For the years ahead FORD has it!

This is the Ford Tudor—America's favorite family car! That Luxury Lifeguard Body is all heavy-gauge steel. Six people can travel in comfort and style because it has more hip and shoulder room than any other car in Ford's price class.

This is the Ford Fordor—admired throughout the land for its all-around usefulness. You could pay a whale of a lot more money and still not get a choice of engines like Ford's famous 100-h.p. V-8 or 95-h.p. Six. What's more, you can have Conventional Drive, Overdrive or brilliant new Fordomatic Drive.

This is the Ford Convertible—a car you can make a roadster or a coupe just by operating the automatic top-control switch. On sunny days and balmy evenings, youngsters and oldsters alike thrill to its top-down "wind in the face" exhilaration . . . but when the weather frowns, it quickly transforms to snug, closed-car coziness at the touch of a button.

This is the Ford Club Coupe—"fashion styled" in every detail and there's a "working" version of it in the Ford Business Coupe. Like all new Fords, both have 43 "Look Ahead" features and are built to see you through the years ahead.

This is the Ford Victoria—the car that gives you the smart styling of a convertible with the snugness of a sedan. It's the belle of the boulevard . . . built especially for those with a yen for distinctive design.

This is the Ford Country Squire. People fondly refer to this station wagon as a "Double Duty Dandy" because it's pretty enough to drive to a ball and roomy enough to haul a sofa or a grove of infant pine trees.

See "Ford Festival" starring James Melton on NBC-TV

You can pay more but you can't buy better than the **FORD**

Every Ford is fashion-designed in a wide variety of exterior colors, with a choice of interior trims color-keyed to achieve an eye-stopping ensemble. And it is built to stay beautiful for the years ahead because the quality is there—in every feature and in every part! "Test Drive" it at your Ford Dealer's now!

1951 FORD

So easy to see...

Kaiser's the car!

1951 Kaiser sedan wins world's highest honor Grand Prix d'Honneur Cannes, France

1951 Kaiser ...the only car with Anatomic Design!

1951 Kaiser DeLuxe 4-Door Sedan. One of 6 body styles, 12 models. Hydra-Matic drive available in all models at extra cost.

So pleasing to the eye . . . so easy to see out of! The new 1951 Kaiser gives more windshield and window area than any other passenger car . . . 1096 square inches in the windshield *alone*! The slim, slant-back corner posts eliminate "blind spots"...give you Kaiser's Control-Tower Vision...one of the many features of Kaiser's Anatomic Design that increase your safety, comfort, convenience!

Winner of the Grand Prize of Honor at Cannes, France, the 1951 Kaiser offers *everything* you've ever desired in a fine motor car. And everything is designed for the years ahead! Feature for feature, the 1951 Kaiser is the newest thing on wheels—in styling...engineering ...and comfort! See it at your Kaiser-Frazer dealer's now!

1951 KAISER DE LUXE FOUR-DOOR SEDAN

Name your price! Name your power!

Then pick your '51 HUDSON

from these 4 rugged series...

The fabulous HUDSON HORNET Series
powered by the sensational, new H-145 engine

PLUS HYDRA-MATIC DRIVE*

Tune in THE BILLY ROSE SHOW
ABC-TV Network

FROM the lower-priced Pacemaker to the fabulous Hudson Hornet, every Hudson brings you streamlined Skyliner Styling—and all the advantages of Hudson's "step-down" design.

This exclusive design, with its recessed floor, makes Hudson the lowest-built American car. You get the most room in any car . . . the lowest center of gravity for the world's best and safest ride . . . full road clearance, too.

Skyliner Styling also means rich, new interiors! No matter which Hudson you choose, you'll discover luxury and convenience beyond anything at or near its price!

Four great engines power the Hudsons for '51—every one packed with satin-smooth, high-compression power—every one built to *outlast* and *outperform* any engine in its class.

How about visiting your Hudson dealer—making *your* choice?

Hydra-Matic Drive optional at extra cost on all Hudson Hornet and Commodore Custom Series models. Super-matic Drive available at extra cost on Super-Six Custom and Pacemaker Custom Series.

The luxurious COMMODORE Custom Series
Your choice of high-compression, high-output Super-Six or the even more powerful Super-Eight engine.

The renowned SUPER-SIX Custom Series
Powered by the famous high-compression, high-output Super-Six engine.

The lower-priced PACEMAKER Custom Series
Glamorous styling plus step-away performance with the high-compression Pacemaker-Six engine.

PRICES START FROM JUST ABOVE THE LOWEST!

1951 HUDSON

the car for today! ...The *Henry J*

America's most important new car!

The *Henry J* DeLuxe sedan...See it today at your Kaiser-Frazer dealer's!

costs less to buy ... less to drive ... less to maintain!

smart !

Timely as this very second, with a new Windsweep design that's as smart as it's practical and as comfortable as it's smart...with new speed-style radiator grille and fluted upswept fenders...roomy, double-purpose interior that converts to give you 51 cubic feet of storage space!

tough !

Yes, tough as an ox! Husky Double-Channel Frame reinforced like a steel bridge...shorter turning radius for easiest parking... Triple-Control Steering and oversized brakes for easiest, safest handling! Ruggedly built for long-lasting service.

thrifty !

Up to 30-35 miles a gallon from its smooth, responsive Supersonic Engines (Henry J—4 cylinders; Henry J DeLuxe—6 cylinders). Saves on maintenance...repairs...operating cost...yes, even insurance! Come in and let us *prove* its amazing economy—now!

and nimble as a kitten !

Built to Better the Best on the Road!

Kaiser-Frazer Sales Corporation, Willow Run, Michigan

1951 KAISER-FRAZER

Exciting to look at__thrilling to drive !

Lincoln

for 1951

1951 LINCOLN

1951
MERCURYS

"Nothing like it for *Style!*"

It has a beauty that's more than skin-deep—and it's built to stay in style for years to come!

For long-lasting style, the 1951 Mercury is the car to see and be seen in! You enjoy better see-ability, too. Mercury's new rear window for instance has more than 1000 square inches of broad view.

There's breath-taking new styling inside as well. New, long-wearing upholstery fabrics are part of the 1951 Mercury value story—give it a truly beautiful air.

Here's an outstanding performer, too. The 1951 Mercury provides just the right balance between new Hi-compression power and road-hugging stability. That precision balance means more hours of power-packed motoring satisfaction.

Mercury is just tops for all-round value! You get more car for your money—more resale value—spend less on gasoline and maintenance. Once you've driven one, you won't settle for anything less than a new 1951 Mercury.

Better see your Mercury Dealer today. Find out why the 1951 Mercury is truly "the buy of your life!"

MERCURY DIVISION · FORD MOTOR COMPANY

New 1951! **MERCURY**
Nothing like it on the *Road!*

3-WAY CHOICE! For "the drive of your life," Mercury now proudly makes available a triple choice in transmissions: Merc-O-Matic Drive, the new, simpler, smoother, more efficient automatic transmission—or thrifty Touch-O-Matic Overdrive are optional at extra cost. There's also silent-ease synchronized standard transmission.

---

① *Road Test It!* MERCURY

Standard equipment, accessories, and trim illustrated are subject to change without notice.

PICK OUT YOUR OWN PROVING GROUND and convince yourself. You'll be amazed at the nimble way Mercury needles its way through the heaviest traffic—at the ease with which it irons out the heaviest traffic—and when it comes to great performance, there's nothing like it on the road. Yes, you really have to drive this great car—put it through its paces—to convince yourself. Drive a Mercury and drive a bargain!

② *Budget Test It!*

PRICE	ECONOMY	LONG LIFE
You can understand Mercury's price tag—a big dollar's worth for every dollar invested.	Mercury has proved its more-miles-per-gallon by winning officially sponsored tests.	92% of all Mercurys built for use in U. S. are still on the road, according to official registrations.

UPKEEP	TRADE-IN	VALUE
You save money year after year. Mercury's stamina keeps repairs at a rock-bottom low.	Mercurys keep their value: used-car market reports prove it. Ask your dealer to show you.	Solid value, say Mercury owners! So will you when you get the story from your dealer!

3-WAY CHOICE! For "the drive of your life!" Mercury now proudly makes available a triple choice in transmissions. Merc-O-Matic Drive, the new simpler, smoother, more efficient automatic transmission—or thrifty Touch-O-Matic Overdrive are optional at extra cost. There's also silent-ease standard transmission.

MAKE THE **MERCURY** 2-WAY TEST—for *"the buy of your life!"*

I BUY ANY BUDGET!
NOW I KNOW WHY MERCURY IS SO POPULAR

It's SMART to ride the "Rocket"!

Smarter looking! Smarter riding! Smarter driving! It's Oldsmobile's all-new, all-time great—the Super "88" for 1951! Look over the superb new styling of this dramatic new car. Relax in the luxury of the bigger, wider, smarter Body by Fisher. Test the flashing power, the smooth, swift response of the new gas-saving "Rocket" Engine! Thrill to the silken-soft ride of Oldsmobile's all-new chassis . . . the magic driving ease of new Oldsmobile Hydra-Matic*. Only then will you know: you're found a new and smarter way to go . . . in Oldsmobile's sensational new Super "88"!

SUPER "88"

"ROCKET" **OLDSMOBILE**

Above, Oldsmobile Super "88" Holiday Coupé. *Hydra-Matic Drive optional at extra cost. Equipment, accessories, and trim illustrated subject to change without notice.

A GENERAL

Ride the "Rocket" and Save!

Master of the miles and miser with your money—that's Oldsmobile's all-new Super "88"! Thrilling action plus exceptional economy are yours in this newest "Rocket" Engine car! What's more, the Super "88" gives you Oldsmobile's sweeping new styling—Oldsmobile's wonderful new ride—and even more effortless motoring with Oldsmobile's new Hydra-Matic Drive*! The great new Body by Fisher is more spacious and luxurious. Major advancements have made the famous high-compression "Rocket" Engine more economical than ever! Try the new Super "88" and you'll know why: you save when you ride the "Rocket"!

SUPER "88"

"ROCKET" **OLDSMOBILE**

Above, Oldsmobile Super "88" 2-Door Sedan. *Hydra-Matic Drive optional at extra cost. Equipment, accessories, and trim illustrated subject to change without notice.

PRODUCT OF GENERAL MOTORS

1951 OLDSMOBILE SUPER "88" HOLIDAY
COUPE AND TWO-DOOR SEDAN

WORLD PREMIERE

OF A DARING NEW CONCEPT IN MOTOR CARS!

★ New concept of functional beauty with . . . New low-to-the-road styling! New Guide-line fenders! New Horizon-view visibility! Stunning new, roomier, Fashion Forum interiors!

★ New concept of performance . . . New Packard Thunderbolt engines combine with 1951 Packard Ultramatic Drive to give you America's most advanced traffic-and-highway performance—with spectacular new economy!

Above: PACKARD PATRICIAN '400'   —one of nine exciting new models for '51

★ New concept of restful riding with . . . New Hush-toned soundproofing! New Load-ease steering! New Broad-beam suspension—a wonderful new feature of Packard's famed Limousine Ride!

★ New concept of safety with . . . [unclear] rib body construction!

★ Above all: It's more than a car, [unclear]kard— [unclear] this your [unclear]wns one!"

NEW, ALL-NEW
1951 PACKARD
—the one for '51!

1951 Packard Patrician "400"

Wonderful—in Sunlight or Moonlight!   **1951 Pontiacs**

1952 Chevrolet

1952 CHEVROLET

See what an exciting selection is yours in Chevrolet for '52!

A model to strike every fancy and suit every need . . . 26 brilliant new colors and two-tone color combinations with new color-matched interiors in all De Luxe sedans and Coupes! Smarter looking, smoother running, softer riding . . . and again in 1952, the lowest-priced line in its field!

You'd never guess by looking that Chevrolet for '52 is the lowest-priced line in its field. Styling is more outstanding than ever . . . and the new color-harmonizing interiors make the selection of your

over-all color scheme as exciting as decorating your home. You'd never dream, by driving it, that this fine, big car is so economical to buy and keep up. New Centerpoise Power "screens out" vibration and power impulses to bring you wonderful new freedom from vibration and road shock . . . and new shock absorber action makes the ride even smoother and softer. You wouldn't expect simpler, smoother Power-glide* automatic transmission, teamed with the most powerful valve-in-head engine in its field, to carry the smallest price tag in its field. But it does. See your Chevrolet dealer, pick your model and pocket your savings! America will confirm your choice for more people buy Chevrolets than any other car. Chevrolet Division of General Motors, Detroit 2, Michigan.

*Combination of Powerglide automatic transmission and extra-powerful valve-in-head engine with new Automatic Choke optional on De Luxe models at extra cost.

The Only Fine Cars
PRICED SO LOW!

CHEVROLET

Smoothie

1952 CHEVROLET STYLELINE DE LUXE TWO-DOOR SEDAN

DeSoto
Fire Dome 8

You've heard about its amazing 160 h.p. V-8 performance... *Full* Power Steering, Power Braking and America's finest No-Shift Driving. Now go and try it for *yourself!* Today!

MORE POWER from every drop of gas! Fire Dome... America's most advanced engine design... gives you sensational performance on *regular fuel!*

EASY AS DIALING a phone . . . De Soto Full (*not partial*) Power Steering makes parking that simple! And road control is greater at all speeds.

AMERICA'S FINEST No-Shift Driving . . . in both De Soto Fire Dome Eight and De Soto Powermaster Six. Just step on gas to go . . . step on brake to stop!

White sidewall tires, when avail-

1952 DeSotos, Fire Dome 8

The New
DeSoto
Fire Dome 8

With its mighty 160 h.p. V-Eight Engine... Power Steering... Power Braking... and No-Shift Driving... it is the most revolutionary new car of 1952. See and *drive* it!

Drive...AS NEVER BEFORE!
This Fire Dome engine with famous dome-shaped combustion chambers gets more power from every drop of fuel. Terrific acceleration and cruising performance on *regular gas.* ★★★★ Smart, practical Air-Vent Hood directs stream of cool air to carburetor for maximum engine power.

Steer...WITHOUT EFFORT!
Power Steering is easy as dialing a telephone . . . you can turn wheel with one finger. Hydraulic power does the work. Parking is easy!
DE SOTO DIVISION, CHRYSLER CORPORATION

White sidewall tires, when available, are optional equipment.

"My, the neighbors sure like our New '52 Dodge!"

1952 Dodge Coronet Sierra Four-Door Station Wagon

"but darling... they're staring at our new '52 Dodge"

Drive the very new,
very beautiful '52 Dodge

Enjoy greater all 'round visibility, smoother riding, extra roominess, the pride and satisfaction of having spent your money wisely and well.

Big, new, dependable **'52 DODGE**

Specifications and equipment subject to change without notice.

1952 Dodge Coronet Diplomat

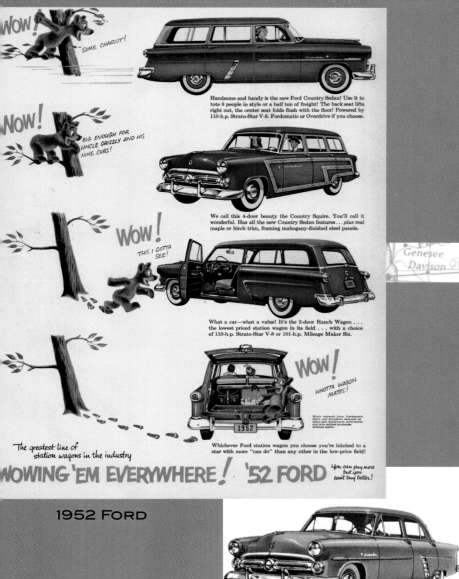

1952 FORD

WOWING 'EM EVERYWHERE! '52 FORD You can pay more but you cant buy better!

1952 FORD
SUNLINER
CONVERTIBLE,
VICTORIA

1952 FORD

1952 HUDSON HORNET

of Kaiser's Anatomic Engineering... **the New '52 Kaiser** *Manhattan*

New 4-Door '52 Kaiser Manhattan. Styled like a hardtop, priced like a sedan! White wall tires extra when available.

1. Slant-back corner posts—narrower—no "blind spots"!
2. One-piece Safety-Mounted Windshield— designed to push outward upon severe impact!

See the world's safest front seat!

America's Most Advanced New Car
At last, you and your family can drive with real peace of mind! For, thanks to Kaiser's advanced Anatomic Engineering," you now can relax in the *safest front seat* ever created for an automobile!

Safety engineers...doctors...insurance experts will acclaim this brilliant safety feature—one of many of Kaiser's great advancements for 1952! Combined with it are Kaiser's *smoother* new Flying Shadow Ride...*lowest* center of gravity for greater roadability...*easier* new Curve-Master steering...*largest* glass area of any sedan...largest Panoramic one-piece windshield...*thriftier* new Supersonic power...*luxurious* new "custom" interiors!

What's more, you enjoy all this – plus Kaiser's handsome new "hardtop" styling at sedan prices! So..."take off the blinders" and look at the new '52 Kaiser today! You'll see why it's your *safest buy today!* You'll discover that Kaiser's Anatomic Engineering gives you a *better* and *more beautiful* car for your money! *Phone your Kaiser•Frazer dealer for a demonstration now!*

Kaiser's Anatomic (Ana-TOM-ic) Engineering: the newest, most advanced step in motor car making. The principle of engineering the anatomy of the car to suit the needs of human anatomy!

1952 KAISER MANHATTAN

LINCOLN —
for the fine art of modern living

MAKING AN ENTRANCE IN MODERN STYLE. Lincoln's 3,271 square inches of glass give modern, glass-wall visibility. Modern Fiberglas insulation hushes your ride. And Lincoln's completely new overhead valve V-8 engine is effortlessly controlled with new HYDRA-MATIC Transmission and new ball-joint front wheel suspension.

EXHIBITING THE SPACIOUSNESS OF MODERN LIVING. And magnificent Lincoln expresses it in motion. There is driving luxury with divan-width seats, deep-pile carpeting, and sparkling new appointments. And you can enrich the interior from an almost wanton selection of colorful fabrics and leathers.

Standard equipment, accessories, and trim illustrated are subject to change without notice. Sea-tint glass and white side-wall tires optional at extra cost.

1952 LINCOLN

This One Challenges Them All

TAKE a long, lingering look at this new 1952 Mercury. For it's new from the inside out— a car that challenges the automobile world to match it . . . a car that challenges you to drive it. That new Forerunner Styling grew out of 10 years' research, dares to be different. The results? Stirring new lines, live weight not dead weight, 17% greater visibility, and Space-Planned interiors. And that famous Mercury high-compression power is yours in even greater measure. For there's a far-advanced 125-hp. V-8 engine, the latest and finest in a line of action-packed economy champions. One look—one road test—and you'll never settle for less. See your Mercury dealer today.

MERCURY DIVISION • FORD MOTOR COMPANY

Standard equipment, accessories, and trim illustrated are subject to change without notice. White wall tires, and seat-tint glass, optional at extra cost.

THE NEW 1952
MERCURY
WITH MERC-O-MATIC DRIVE

3-WAY CHOICE of transmissions: Merc-O-Matic Drive and thrifty Touch-O-Matic Overdrive are optional at extra cost. Also available, silent-ease standard transmission.

1952 MERCURY

NEW POWER FOR SMOOTH CRUISING. Premium product of the most experienced builders of V-8's, Lincoln's new engine features overhead valves, Hi-swirl combustion chambers, 7.5 to 1 compression ratio. Effortless handling through new dual-range steering. Transmission— and new ball-joint front wheel suspension, first on any U. S. production car.

STYLING IN STEP WITH THE HOMES OF TODAY. Designed for those who live behind glass walls, Lincoln is the fine car that lets a man (or a girl) see where he (or she) is going, with new wide visibility (3,271 square inches all around with sea-tint glass available) and compact see-ahead hood. New principles of body construction permit chair-high seating, much more leg and head room. New concepts of styling introduce dramatic body lines, sumptuous interiors.

Now— *Lincoln*
puts *modern* living on wheels

Standard equipment, accessories, and trim illustrated are subject to change without notice. White wall tires optional at extra cost.

1952 LINCOLN

Take Charge of the Car

NEW PERFORMANCE
NEW DESIGN

New Interceptor Panel brings all controls within easy reach. Smooth Merc-O-Matic Drive* and advanced 125-hp V-8 put you in command of the road. New modern design results in *live* weight not dead weight.

That Challenges Them All

Find out why Mercury is Winning New Friends and Influencing Old Customers

BEFORE you even start the advanced V-8 engine you know that here is something *really* new. Now, you can *see* over the hood, down front, to each fender. There's move-around comfort to spare! There's Forerunner Styling—sweeping, jet-lined grace—space-planned from the inside out to put you, the motorist, first on the *American Road*. And Mercury's famous V-8, that has won official economy tests two years in a row, now has far greater horsepower with the high-compression performance that you'd expect from the maker of more V-8 engines than all others combined.

This is Mercury for 1952 . . . challenging the automotive world . . . challenging *you* to drive it. Let your dealer prove it.

MERCURY DIVISION   FORD MOTOR COMPANY

The New 1952
MERCURY
WITH MERC-O-MATIC DRIVE

*3-WAY CHOICE of transmissions: Merc-O-Matic Drive and Thrifty Touch-O-Matic Overdrive are optional at extra cost. Also available, silent-ease standard transmission.

1952 MERCURY

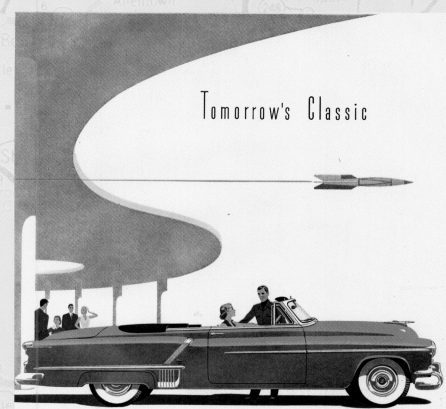

Tomorrow's Classic

Oldsmobile Ninety-Eight Convertible. A General Motors Product

*Hydra-Matic Super Drive, GM Hydraulic Steering, Autronic-Eye, white sidewall tires (when available) optional at extra cost. Equipment, accessories, and trim illustrated subject to change without notice.

1952 Oldsmobile Ninety-Eight Convertible

Johnny and Lucille, Oldsmobile's singing sweethearts, invite you to ride the "Rocket" . . . to drive Oldsmobile's sensational new Super "88"!

TRY 160 H.P.
"ROCKET" ACTION
. . . in the New Super "88"

You've got to drive it to believe it! Never before has Oldsmobile had such an exciting performance story to tell! For here is a *new* kind of "Rocket" Engine car—*dramatically new* with the flashing 160-horsepower "Rocket" . . . now paired with smooth new Hydra-Matic Super Drive*! The result is performance that truly *stands out* even in this era of high-powered motor cars! GM Hydraulic Steering*, the amazing Autronic-Eye*, and a host of other new features add to your comfort and safety. Drive Oldsmobile's Super "88" once and you'll never settle for anything else!

*Above, Oldsmobile Super "88" 2-Door Sedan. *Hydra-Matic Super Drive, GM Hydraulic Steering, Autronic-Eye and white sidewall tires (when available) optional at extra cost. Equipment, accessories and trim, subject to change without notice.   A General Motors Value

"ROCKET" POWERED OLDSMOBILE

The Whole World looks up to the "Rocket"!

Oldsmobile's famous singing sweethearts invite you along for the world's top motoring thrill—an Oldsmobile "Rocket Ride"!

"ROCKET"!—a magic name to more than a million Oldsmobile owners!
"ROCKET"!—flashing new high-compression power at its very best!
"ROCKET"!—drive the sensational Super "88" for your once-in-a-lifetime "Rocket" thrill! Experience the smooth, swift surge of "Rocket" Engine power as it teams with Hydra-Matic Super Drive*! Thrill to the effortless ease of GM Hydraulic Steering*—the amazing convenience of the Autronic-Eye*, Oldsmobile's automatic headlight dimmer! Come ride the "Rocket"—there's nothing else like it! Make *your* date with Oldsmobile's brilliant new Super "88"!

SUPER "88"

*Above, Oldsmobile Super "88" 4-Door Sedan. *Hydra-Matic Super Drive, GM Hydraulic Steering, Autronic-Eye, optional at extra cost. Equipment, accessories and trim, subject to change without notice. Product of General Motors.

"ROCKET" OLDSMOBILE

1952 Oldsmobile Super "88" Two-Door Sedans

PACKARD

Now Better In 70 Ways...With Exclusive Ultramatic, The Automatic Drive That Outperforms Them All!

More Than 53% Of All Packards Built Since 1899 Are Still In Use!

1952 PACKARD

It's just <u>wonderful</u> to drive!

Spectacular—that's the only word for it!

1952 PONTIACS

Sunshine and Pleasure in Every Mile!

*S*tar of the silky way

THIS one had to be good. It's our Golden Anniversary ROADMASTER. So upon it we lavished our skills, our talents and our time to make it the finest in a fifty-year line of fine cars.

When you drive it, you will come to know how good a fifty-year best really is.

You'll know it in the swift and soaring power response of its V8 Engine. The first Fireball V8. The first such V8 with 8.5 to 1 compression, with vertical valves, with 12-volt electrical system, with a host of modern engineering features.

You'll know it in the silken velocity of its getaway — with Twin-Turbine Dynaflow adding far swifter, quieter acceleration to infinite smoothness.

You'll know it, too, in the velvety luxury of its bettered ride, in the new ease of its handling, in the more precise control it gives you, in the more reassuring comfort you feel.

For Buick engineers pulled all the stops on this 1953 ROADMASTER. They widened the front tread — compacted the frame — shortened the turn radius — recalibrated the four coil springs — increased the braking power — made

Power Steering standard equipment, and even added Power Brakes* to lighten the task of quick, sure stopping.

But why say more?

It is for you, the beneficiary of all this engineering excellence, to discover the great and gorgeous going of the swiftest, the smoothest, the silkiest, the most silent automobile yet built in half a century of Buick building.

Your Buick dealer will be happy to introduce you two. Why not visit him soon?
BUICK *Division of* GENERAL MOTORS
*Optional at extra cost.

Then—
Now—
Tomorrow

1903
1953

When better automobiles are built BUICK will build them

Custom Built **ROADMASTER** *by Buick*

1953 BUICK

1953 BUICK

1953 CHEVROLET TWO-TEN FOUR-DOOR SEDAN, BEL AIR SPORT COUPE

1953 CHEVROLET TWO-TEN FOUR DOOR SEDAN

1953 CHEVROLET BEL AIR TWO-DOOR SEDAN

Chrysler New Yorker DeLuxe 4-door Sedan

Now on display

AMERICA'S FIRST FAMILY OF FINE CARS

Chrysler New Yorker DeLuxe Convertible—New Yorker and New Yorker DeLuxe in 9 body styles

A stunning new mood in Highway Fashion!

Never before has such a brilliant array of fine motor cars been introduced to the American public . . . styled to create a glamorous new mood in Highway Fashion . . . and embodying the kind of engineering the world associates with Chrysler performance and Chrysler safety!

And here is a *range* of cars unequalled anywhere. The beautiful Windsor line . . . lowest-priced of all Chryslers. The spectacular New Yorker . . . whose performance has all America talking. The matchless Imperial . . . custom-built for those who demand the absolute finest. All in a variety of body models, colors, and interior trim combinations to suit every need and every wish.

. . . and now on display at your nearby Chrysler dealer's!

The beautiful 1953

CHRYSLER

Chrysler Custom Imperial 4-door Sedan—Imperial line also includes the Town Limousine

Chrysler Windsor Club Coupe—Windsor and Windsor DeLuxe in 7 body styles

1953 CHRYSLER

As distinguished in performance as in appearance, with Full Power Steering, Power Braking and the World's Most Powerful Engine Design!

THE *Distinguished De Soto*

FOR 1953

It's the most beautiful De Soto ever built. Every line, every curve, every detail is new, from air-vent hood to jet tail lights, from one-piece curved windshield to sweep-around rear window.

Sensational Power

Expect incomparable performance, whether you choose the mighty 160 h.p. Fire Dome V-8 or the economical De Soto Powermaster Six.

Full Power Steering

Here's the most wonderful car improvement since the self-starter. Makes

driving safer, easier under all conditions. And it makes parking as easy as dialing a telephone.

No-Shift Driving

This De Soto offers effortless No-Shift Driving — Power Braking — Oriflow Shock Absorbers — Safety-Rim Wheels — Chair-High Seats — dozens of other outstanding features.

Now on Display

This beautiful new De Soto is now on display at your De Soto dealer's. See and drive it soon. It will be an unforgettable experience.

De Soto Division, Chrysler Corp.

DeSoto *Famous for Fine Engineering*

The 160 h.p. FIRE DOME V8 • The POWERMASTER 6

1953 DESOTO

US 114

CORONET V-EIGHT 4-DOOR SEDAN

The Action Car for Active Americans

CORONET V-EIGHT CONVERTIBLE COUPE

CORONET V-EIGHT CLUB COUPE

CORONET V-EIGHT DIPLOMAT

1953 DODGE

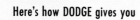

Here's how DODGE gives you
New Mastery of the Road!

Powerful! Thrifty! The nimblest car on the highway!

Come discover for yourself the great Dodge V-Eight that *outperformed all other 8's* in the Mobilgas Economy Run. Test the reserve of safety-power that gets more action from every drop of gasoline. Feel the new maneuverability and handling ease that make light of traffic. See how Dodge snugs down on curves like a true sports car. It's all yours... at new lower prices...in the sensational new Dodge—

The Action Car for Active Americans

On Hills — Your 140-h.p. Red Ram V-8 engine takes grades in stride. There's no strain, no labor! You always feel you have power to spare—and on "regular" gasoline, too! Dodge is America's top economy 8.

In Passing — Your Dodge V-8 provides you with a magnificent reserve of power to help you pass cars more safely, more confidently. And Gyro-Torque Drive with "Scat" gear really jumps you ahead.

On Curves — You enjoy a new sense of control. New "Stabilizer" suspension cuts sway, tames roll. Chassis is action-designed, more rigid and rugged. Oriflow ride-control levels the road for comfort and safety.

Dependable

DODGE
V-Eight or Six

Mobilgas Economy Winner — Dodge tops all other 8's in the famous 1206-mile Mobilgas Economy Run! Over winding mountain roads, on high-speed highways, through city traffic ... the Dodge V-8 proved its economical mastery of the road.

Specifications and equipment subject to change without notice

1953 DODGE CORONET V-EIGHT CONVERTIBLE

Beauty is only <u>half</u> the picture!

Fifty Years Forward on the American Road

1953 FORD

You get "Worth More" Convenience
Ford has the biggest luggage compartment in its field. Deck lid opens at a key turn on counterbalancing hinges.

You get "Worth More" Economy
Both V-8 and Six have Ford's gas-saving Automatic Power Pilot for high-compression performance with regular gas.

1953 FORDS

NEW <u>kind</u> of car in the lowest price field

ECONOMICAL as a Scot

COMPACT, a delight to handle, drive and park

Exquisite as a jewel case... quick and powerful as a panther

HUDSON *JET*

1953 HUDSON JET

1 PERFORMANCE comparable <u>only</u> to the fabulous Hudson Hornet !

2 ECONOMY better than anything you've ever seen in the low-price field !

1953 HUDSON HORNET

This Is The News That Got Around

1953 KAISER MANHATTAN

1953 Kaiser Manhattan 4-door sedan. White sidewall tires and Dual-Range Hydra-Matic optional at extra cost.

1953 KAISER MANHATTAN FOUR-DOOR SEDAN

PACKARD

Two Great New Lines of Cars for '53!

The Luxurious PACKARD
America's New Choice In The Fine-Car Field!

FROM America's oldest builder of fine automobiles comes a great new car in the quality field —PACKARD for '53. With the world's highest-compression eight, Packard provides more power than you will ever use . . . plus the industry's finest no-shift drive, power steering, and power brakes proved in over a full year of actual use!

IF YOU WANT a truly *distinctive* car, and want it *now*, see America's most *advanced* car—with trend-setting contour styling, with effortless ease of handling and with the smooth, silent comfort of the famous Packard ride. More than 50 per cent of all Packards built since 1899 are still in use—proof that "Built like a Packard" means really *built to last!*

NOW . . . ASK THE MAN WHO OWNS ONE

The New Packard CLIPPER
Big-Car Value At Medium-Car Cost!

NOW PACKARD offers an entirely new line in a wide range of advanced contour-styled models —the new *Packard CLIPPERS—for big-car value at medium-car cost.* These true products of Packard experience, engineering and skill give you *real Packard quality*, inside and out, for just a few hundred dollars more than cars in the *low*-priced field.

POWERED BY PACKARD's mighty Thunderbolt Eight Engines, they are the roomiest cars in their price class—with seats as wide as these cars are high and with the largest luggage compartment of any sedan. So no matter what you may plan to spend for a car, PACKARD—with *two* great new lines for '53—offers you your *best motorcar investment.*

1953 PACKARD CLIPPER

1953 PACKARD CARIBBEAN

For a Rocketing Good Time . . .

Take off for the kick-off in a "Rocket" Holiday! It's the *best seat* to the game . . . the *best seat* to go *anywhere* for that matter! You'll thrill to the surging might of Oldsmobile's magnificent "Rocket" Engine! You'll marvel at the ease of Power Steering* for turning, parking . . . at the swift, sure, effortless response of Oldsmobile Power Brakes*. Best of all, you'll ride in a car whose gay spirit fits every gala day . . . a flashing Super "88" Holiday!

*Optional at extra cost.

Car illustrated above: Super "88" Holiday Coupé. A General Motors Value.

"ROCKET" ENGINE

1953 OLDSMOBILE SUPER "88"
HOLIDAY COUPE

summer classic

Tops for the "top-down" days ahead . . . the Classic Ninety-Eight Convertible by Oldsmobile. It's youthful, gay, carefree—and styled to *look* the part. Rakish lines and bold contours are gracefully proportioned to achieve true Classic design. What's more, this spirited beauty *acts* the part, with the smooth, hushed response of the mighty "Rocket" Engine, with effortless Power Steering* and Pedal-Ease Power Brakes*. You're cordially invited to drive this Classic Convertible. Visit your Oldsmobile Dealer soon.

*Optional at extra cost.

*Car illustrated above:
Ninety-Eight Convertible Coupé.
A General Motors Value.*

"ROCKET" ENGINE

OLDSMOBILE

1953 OLDSMOBILE NINETY-EIGHT
CONVERTIBLE COUPE

88

Heads Up! FOR '53...
HERE COMES
OLDSMOBILE!

THE BIG "FEATURE CAR" OF THE YEAR

with New Power Brakes,
Power Steering,
and Power Styling, too!

This is the car you've been waiting for . . . the "power" car of the year! It's *Oldsmobile*—the *sensational, all-new Super "88" Oldsmobile*—most beautiful, most powerful ever built! Here's the car that's packed with more "power" features than you've ever seen in any automobile! New "Rocket" Engine—a higher-power, higher-compression, higher-voltage "Rocket" Engine for dependence

New Pedal-Ease Power Brakes* for quicker, surer stopping power! New Power-Ride Chassis —more rigid, more rugged for a smoother, softer ride! Power Steering* for safer, easier parking, turning, maneuvering! New Power Styling with a new long, level fender line— bold new front end—brilliant new chrome trim! All in all, it's the "Big Feature" car of the

Optional at extra cost. Car illustrated above: Oldsmobile Super "88" Holiday Coupe. New Classic Ninety-Eight also now on display at your dealer's.

1953 OLDSMOBILE SUPER "88" HOLIDAY COUPE

The Plymouth Cranbrook Sedan and the Plymouth Savoy, shown at the Greenbrier, White Sulphur Springs, W. Va.

The architecture of an automobile can kindle a light in its owner's eyes and warm the pride of possession. As, indeed, the balanced new beauty of the Plymouth does. And beneath this beauty, unseen, is the integrity of the engineering that created it . . . a low-priced car, built so well, to look so well, to serve so long and well.

PLYMOUTH

1953 PLYMOUTH CRANBROOK SEDAN, SAVOY

The Plymouth Belvedere, shown at the Challenger Inn, Sun Valley, Idaho.

It seems the sun always shines on those who drive Plymouths. For when a car looks right, rides right and serves you faithfully through the miles, you can't help but take great pleasure from owning it. Because there's more quality built into a Plymouth, you are sure to get more lasting value out of it.

PLYMOUTH

1953 PLYMOUTH BELVEDERE

It's only human to get a glow when others view your car with admiring eyes.
The satisfaction of Plymouth owners doesn't end here. For they know
that their car contains admirable traits you can't see in a glance—
advanced engineering, quality materials, honest craftsmanship, and an enduring
performance that constantly sustains their judgment in choosing a Plymouth.

PLYMOUTH

Chrysler Corporation's No. 1 Car

1953 PLYMOUTH CRANBROOK CONVERTIBLE CLUB COUPE

1953 Pontiac

More than the grace of greatness

1954 Buick Roadmaster

1954 Buick Roadmaster

1954 Buick Skylark

1954 BUICK

You're only young _twice_!

1954 CHEVROLET BEL AIR SPORT COUPE

Like 'em lively, graceful and dashing?

1954 CHEVROLET BEL AIR CONVERTIBLE

1954 CHEVROLET DELRAY COUPE

Announcing '54 DODGE
Elegance in Action

Specifications, equipment and price subject to change without notice.

DODGE ROYAL V-8 FOUR DOOR SEDAN

The Dodge with more than ever before!

More to it—More in it—More of it!

There is a fresh beauty to the new '54 Dodge . . . a gracious elegance that brings even greater rewards of driving pleasure and satisfaction to the car now famous as the Action Car for Active Americans. Dodge 1954 Première Week—starts October 8.

New Fully Automatic PowerFlite Drive is newest, smoothest, most powerful of all automatic transmissions. No clutch—just press the accelerator for a surging flow of velvet power.

New Red Ram 150 V-8 . . . the engine that topped all 8's in the famous Mobilgas Economy Run, set new official AAA performance records—now stepped up to 150 horsepower.

New Full Time Power Steering takes the hard work out of driving—leaves all the pleasure in! You drive more safely, more confidently. You park, take turns with effortless ease.

Elegant Jacquard Fabrics, loomed in the manner of the most exquisite tapestries . . .

DEPENDABLE *New* '54 **DODGE**
The Action Car For Active Americans

1954 DODGE ROYAL V-8 FOUR-DOOR SEDAN

1954 FORD

Mainline

Customline

CLUB COUPE
Like all Customline models, this personal beauty has beautiful new upholstery fabrics and trim in shades color-keyed to match exteriors.

Heavenly Bodies with worlds of Power

The Crestline Victoria, more beautiful than ever is stealing America's heart! You'll find new interiors with a choice of six beautiful new nylon and nylon-and-vinyl upholstery color schemes.

The new Crestline Skyliner is another Ford first in styling. A new tinted transparent roof panel gives an open-car feeling never before achieved in any low-priced closed car.

The Crestline Sunliner is America's largest-selling convertible! Among its '54 advantages you have a choice of four top colors. Also available is a top with a transparent panel over the driver.

130-h.p. Y-block V-8
New deep block is more rigid for smoother operation. Short-stroke design means greater gas economy, longer life. Free-turning overhead valves keep compression high.

RANCH WAGON
With Stownaway seat up, it's a roomy 6-passenger sedan. With seat and tail gate down, there's nearly 8 feet of level load length.

COUNTRY SEDAN
A 4-door, eight-passenger beauty. Two-section center seat folds into floor and rear seat lifts out easily for ample load space.

You can have just the kind of car you want in a Ford!

With 3 distinctive lines . . . 14 brilliant body styles . . . 2 new engines . . .
3 transmissions and 4 optional power assists* to choose from . . .
Ford offers you just the car to suit your needs and tastes.

Choose any Ford you like and you'll enjoy recognized style leadership—modern, clean-lined beauty that "belongs" anywhere!

You'll live "in style" in your '54 Ford surrounded by sparkling new upholstery fabrics and trim. You'll *ride* in extra comfort, too, with Ford's revolutionary new Ball-Joint Front Suspension—the greatest riding advance since independent front wheel suspension. And, with any of Ford's 14 body styles, you can have

either of Ford's two new high-compression overhead valve engines . . . the 130-h.p. Y-block V-8 or the 115-h.p. I-block Six. Both are as modern as tomorrow with advanced overhead-valve, low-friction design for greater economy. And, for those who want the *last* word in driving ease and convenience, Ford offers all the modern power assists.

It's no wonder so many more people are finding *exactly* the kind of car they want in Ford!

Your Ford Dealer cordially invites you to Test Drive the '54 Ford of your choice

Here's the stunning new Crestline Fordor! The ultimate in Fordor styling, it is beautifully appointed throughout. Seats are upholstered in luxurious new nylon fabrics. Two-tone Astra-Dial Control Panel harmonizes with the completely new interior.

Here's the glamorous new Crestline Skyliner! With new transparent roof panel, the new Ford Skyliner is the top hit of the '54 season. With side windows rolled completely down, there's no center post to obstruct your view.

*For the utmost in driving ease and convenience, Ford offers Master-Guide Power Steering, Swift-Sure Power Brakes, Power-Lift Windows and 4-Way Power Seat. Available at extra cost on most models.

Crestline

SKYLINER
Another Ford first in styling! Roof has tinted transparent panel that gives an open-car feeling. Exclusive to Ford in its field.

VICTORIA
For those who want "something special." Side windows roll down completely leaving no center posts. Vinyl or nylon-vinyl upholstery.

FORDOR SEDAN
A distinguished new body style for 1954. Offers new touches in fine-car styling . . . colorful new upholsteries and smartly tailored trim.

SUNLINER
America's favorite convertible. Four two-tone interior combinations complement exterior colors. Tops available in four color-fast shades.

COUNTRY SQUIRE
This 4-door, 8-passenger "double-duty dandy" offers all the beauty of mahogany-grain-finished body panels with blond wood-grained trim.

1954 FORD

US 122

1954 Hudson Hornet

1954 Ford

1954 Oldsmobile
Super "88"
Holiday Coupe

Glamour
that packs a wallop!

Come see the mighty Hornet—and its two great companion cars—at prices starting near the lowest

Here, in the Hornet and in its spectacular running mates, is sheer luxury. Here, too, is a new kind of power from new Instant Action Engines with Super Induction! When you step on it in *any* Hudson, something happens . . . instantly!

GET THE FACTS

Hudson brings you these great advances, not one of which you'll find in any other car at any price:

New Instant Action Engines . . . "Step-down" design with its low center of gravity for a safer, "cling-to-the-road" ride . . . Twin H-Power that develops more action from every drop of gas . . . Flight-Line Styling for true streamlining . . . Triple-Safe Brakes . . . Monobilt body-and-frame¹, most rugged construction known.

Power steering*, power brakes* and fully automatic drives* are also available on most models. You get more for your money in a Hudson. Stop by and see your dealer soon.

*Optional at extra cost.   ¹Trademark. Patented.

Only Y-block V-8 engine in its field—with low-friction design and turbo-wedge combustion chambers for the most advanced V-8 power in the industry

Only Ball-Joint Front Suspension in its field—with weight-tailored. Hydra-Coil Front Springs for a far smoother ride on all roads.

Only car in its field with so many Trend-Setting advancements—such as Center-Fill Fueling, suspended clutch and brake pedals and signal lights for oil and generator.

Only Hulltight Body in its field—with so the roof, floor and hood . . . and all around greater comfort and quiet

Only car in its field with so many features that are found in costliest cars—such as full Hotchkiss drive, riveted brake lining and glass-fibre hood insulation.

Only car in its field with such high resale value. Analysis of used car prices shows that Ford cars return more of their original cost on resale than any competitive car.

— and you'll

GET A FORD

Your Ford Dealer invites you to take a Test Drive

Hudson Hornet Hollywood Hardtop

1954 HUDSON HORNET

HUDSON **WASP**

Spectacular running mate of the Hudson Hornet, gives you Hornet-like glamour and power in the low-medium price field: at a new lower price for 1954.

HUDSON **JET**

Compact, economical edition of the Hornet, with outstanding gas economy and handling ease. Has the amazing roadability of the Hornet. Prices start near the lowest.

THREE OF A KIND . . . in Glamour, Performance and Quality

Everybody looks!
Everybody likes!
looks!

Super "88" Holiday Coupé. A General Motors Value.

Looks lovely . . . looks lively—and it is! For a thrilling lift in your life, we recommend a ride in a "Rocket"! So put yourself in the driver's seat . . . behind that sweeping panoramic windshield . . . and let the "Rocket" take over! You'll cruise more smoothly—steer more easily—pass more safely—stop more surely— when Oldsmobile's out-ahead power features go to work. Ring your dealer for a ride you'll always remember . . . ring for a ride in a "ROCKET 88"!

Be careful—drive safely.

Vision of tomorrow! Panoramic windshield—most-talked-about feature of the year!

Sweep-out fenders and doors give Oldsmobile that new American

Now on Display at Your Dealer's !

Oldsmobile's
"Dream Car"

THE CLASSIC NINETY-EIGHT FOR 1954

Lithe, low rear deck . . . smooth-flowing, sweep-out fenders and doors accentuate the sporting flair of the new Ninety-Eight. Now the driver can see all four fenders for easier parking and safer driving.

Deep foam rubber Custom-Lounge Cushions, Safety-Padded Instrument Panel, Hand Brake Signal and Front Compartment Courtesy Light are new standard equipment on all 1954 DeLuxe Ninety...

More than any model before it, this new "Ninety-Eight" for 1954 expresses Oldsmobile's forward looking and forward thinking. It's Oldsmobile's dream car—the pinnacle toward which Oldsmobile stylists and engineers have been working since the introduction of the "Rocket" Engine. You'll know it as a car of the future by its distinctive panoramic windshield, and the long, low, forward look. And, you'll discover even greater power in the world-famous "Rocket" Engine—185 horsepower and 8.25-to-1 compression ratio. Optional features are Safety Power Steering*, new Power Brakes* and new 4-Way Power Seat Control*. See it now—this ultimate in "Rockets", the magnificent "Ninety-Eight" for 1954—at your Oldsmobile dealer's.

*Optional at extra cost.

Ninety-Eight DeLuxe Holiday Coupé. White sidewall tires optional at extra cost. A General Motors Value.

O L D S M O B I L E

WITH NEW WORLD'S RECORD "ROCKET"

1954 Oldsmobile Ninety-Eight
DeLuxe Holiday Coupe

123

THE STUDEBAKER-PACKARD CORPORATION PRESENTS

The New Packard *Clipper*

For those who want <u>individuality</u> in a medium-price car

Count the people who will find their hearts' desires in the new Clipper! There will be those of instinctive good taste, with an eye for beauty and a feeling for design. There will be sports car enthusiasts who want split-second response at the green light, and power that puts them ahead of the pack on the open road. And there will be those who instantly perceive that this *is* a new kind of medium-price car. Whatever *your* reason for choosing a new Clipper, expect necks to crane and eyes to stare as you dash past. Expect to experience a heart-warming *pride of ownership* in this car *built for people with fine car tastes* by one of the four full-line producers of automotive transportation.

Clipper – the car that makes it smart to be different!

If you hesitate to buy a medium-price car because six months hence it will be "everybody's car" – the new *Clipper is for you!* For in the Clipper you will find the *individuality* you seek . . . and to which you are entitled.

This new Clipper has been expressly designed to be *distinctive* in appearance as well as performance. Every inch a thoroughbred, it is *precision-built* by the Packard Division to traditional Packard standards of quality and good taste. With the big new 225 or 245 HORSEPOWER

CLIPPER V-8 ENGINES, you will command more responsive power than is available in any other car near the Clipper price class. Precision engineering made famous by Packard makes these new Clipper engines compact, quiet models of smooth efficiency.

Clipper's new Twin Ultramatic Transmission . . . two in one . . . gives you a choice of starts . . . lightning get-away . . . ultra smoothness for traffic. Teamed with the new Clipper V-8 engines, it provides outstanding gasoline economy.

New Clipper styling features distinctive sweeping lines. Luxurious interiors offer unlimited choice of harmonious color combinations. The new Clipper is distinguished in its timeless *good taste* . . . it reflects the inimitable Packard touch!

Your Packard dealer invites you to see the new Clipper today. Drive it. Compare it with any car . . . for appearance, for performance, for outstanding value. And you'll agree that the new Packard Clipper gives you distinctive individuality in the medium-price field!

Clipper – Precision-Built by Packard Craftsmen

CLIPPER CONSTELLATION 245 HORSEPOWER

PACKARD TORSION-LEVEL RIDE

1954 Packard Clipper Constellation

1954 Packard Four Hundred

New '54 Plymouth

1954 Plymouths

Even a "bird's-eye view" reveals much of the beauty of the new

1954 **PLYMOUTH**. But to appreciate all the value built into this fine car, you must drive it. Your Plymouth dealer will be happy to arrange

your demonstration – just call or visit him today.

the proudest, most beautiful all-new bring you luxury

A SMOOTH, GLIDING RIDE on any kind of road—yours with Plymouth's Truly Balanced Ride! And with sensationally smooth HY-DRIVE° there's no shifting!

PARKING'S EASY with Plymouth's new full-time POWER STEERING°. It saves your energy in every mile you drive, gives you safer, surer control, with a natural "feel of the road."

TWO WORK BETTER THAN ONE! For smooth, quick, always predictable stops, Plymouth front wheels have two brake cylinders, where other low-price cars have only one.

INTERSTATE

124

1954 Pontiac Star Chief

1954 Studebaker

1955 Buick Special, Century, and
Buick Roadmaster

1955 BUICK

WHEN BETTER AUTOMOBILES ARE BUILT
BUICK WILL BUILD THEM

1955 CADILLAC

1955 CHEVROLET
TWO-TEN
HANDYMAN

1955 CHEVROLET BEL AIR
CONVERTIBLE

The Bel Air Convertible. You'll find your favorite model
among Chevrolet's complete line of Fisher Body beauties.

Already people are saying it's the

smartest of the smart c

It's hard to remember when a new car has caused so
much comment. But it's easy to see why. Barely five feet
high, here's the longest, lowest, widest, most glamorous
De Soto ever built. In any one of 55 color combinations
it has an eye-catching verve and beauty as modern as
tomorrow. All the power you can use and every automatic feature you could want—Powerflite Transmission,
Full-Time Power Steering, Feather-Touch Power Brakes,
Four-Way-Power Front Seat and Air Conditioning.*

See your De Soto dealer and take a turn at the wheel
of "the smartest of the smart cars" today. De Soto
Division, Chrysler Corporation.

*Optional equipment.

TWO MIGHTY V-8's. The famous Firedome increased
to 185 hp, at a new low price. Shown here is the fabulous
Fireflite, a brand-new 200 hp. series.

1955 CHEVROLET

the NEW DE SOTO with the Forward Look

1955 DeSoto
Fireflites

TWO MIGHTY V-8's. The famous Firedome increased to 185 hp, at a
new low price. Shown here is the fabulous Fireflite, a brand-new 200 hp. series.

1955 DeSoto
Sportsman

Smartest of the smart cars

DRIVE A DE SOTO BEFORE YOU DECIDE

CHOOSE FROM 55 COLOR COMBINATIONS.
Here's a Firedome four-door sedan with Dolphin
Blue body and Avon Blue top and color sweep.

This year the famous De Soto Firedome — entirely restyled and
more powerful than ever — comes to you at a new lower price.
This forward-looking, road-hugging beauty has a smartness
that wins admiring glances everywhere. It's so low you can
look right over the roof! And note the New Horizon wrap-
around windshield that is swept back to give you 20 per cent
more glass area.

Both Firedome and Fireflite models have mighty V-8 engines
to give you the thrilling performance De Soto appearance
promises. See — and drive — these "smartest of the smart
cars" at your De Soto dealer before you buy any car! De Soto
Division, Chrysler Corporation.

the NEW DE SOTO with the Forward Look

1955 DeSoto Firedome

The Custom Ranch Wagon. Seats 6
grownups plus cargo. Rear seat folds
down for extra load space. One of
5 stunning station wagons by Ford.

The Fairlane Town Sed
Ford's 16 new body style
styling of the exciting Th

1955 Ford Custom Ranch Wagon,
Fairlane Town Sedan

Seventh heaven on wheels—

the Ford THUNDERBIRD

Wherever—whenever—your Thunderbird ap-
pears in public, the effect is electric. All eyes turn
to its long, low, graceful beauty. All hearts say
"That's for me!"

And if they only knew the full story!

If they could spend but half an hour in *your*
seat. If they could listen to the dual-throated
harmony of its tuned mufflers and twin exhausts.
If they could feel the steepest hills melt before the
might of the 198-h.p. Thunderbird Special V-8.
If they could see the tachometer needle wind up,
as the four-barrel carburetor and 8.5 to 1 compression ratio convert gasoline into road-ruling
Trigger-Torque "Go!"

Then they'd sample a portion of your pride in
your personal car. But you could show them more!

You could show them the way it takes the
corners as if magnetized to the road. You could
let them feel the lightning "take-off" with new
Speed-Trigger Fordomatic Drive. You could show
them how quickly the convertible top whisks into
place — how easily the solid top lifts on and off —
the all-steel body — the ample trunk space — the
rich interiors—the telescoping steering wheel—the
4-way power seat. And should your Thunderbird
have the optional power assists, they could note

the convenience of power steering, power brakes
and power window lifts.

You could show them this and more—how even
routine driving becomes thrilling entertainment.

*Yes, we're day-dreaming for you. But why not
put yourself in the driver's seat and make this dream
come true! The man to see is your Ford Dealer.*

An exciting original by FORD

1955 Ford Thunderbird

Not only does Ford <u>look</u> like the Thunderbird, it <u>behaves</u> like it, too, with Trigger-Torque performance!

A car doesn't always *need* to take off and travel like a well-hit golf ball! But, it's a nice, secure feeling to *know* your Ford has the Trigger-Torque "up-and-at-'em" to do it, should emergency dictate. And it's

also great having a car that *looks* like it's rarin' to go! Ford's long, low, Thunderbird-like lines say "action" in every detail. Such things are especially wonderful when they come at Ford's low prices!

...and going more places!

More and more you see Fords in front of homes where formerly costlier cars were parked!

It's a real satisfaction to know you're piloting a car that's the pride and joy of discriminating owners from Maine to California. And even if you do have money to burn, there's something else about a Ford that will tickle your good business sense. Manufacturer's suggested list prices show that, for about the same cost as plain "do-it-yourself" models of higher priced makes, you can have a distinguished Ford Fairlane with Fordomatic Drive, power steering and brakes, power seat and windows . . . in fact, the works! No wonder so many are going for Ford.

FORD
America's "worth more" car

1955 FORD THUNDERBIRD

THE NEW ULTRA-SMART, LOW SILHOUETTE MONTCLAIR SPORT COUPE

NOW — PICK YOUR NEW MERCURY FROM 11 BEAUTIFUL, SUPER-POWERED MODELS

MONTCLAIR CONVERTIBLE

MONTEREY HARDTOP COUPE

CUSTOM 2-DOOR SEDAN

CUSTOM HARDTOP COUPE

MONTCLAIR 4-DOOR SEDAN

MONTEREY 4-DOOR SEDAN

CUSTOM 4-DOOR SEDAN

CUSTOM 8-PASSENGER STATION WAGON

1955 MERCURY

Fresh as tomorrow's sunrise . . . original as the newest Paris creation . . . yet so completely sensible! One glance tells you this is new, *completely new* . . . a daring, different combination of Holiday grace and 4-door space!

Enter in ease . . . *front compartment or rear!* Four full-size doors open wide, inviting you to a luxury lounge of charm and comfort. And there's no center post to mar the open sweep of Oldsmobile's free-flowing body lines!

1955 OLDSMOBILE HOLIDAY SEDAN

OLDSMOBILE 88 ROCKETS INTO 1955

with Flying Colors!

1955 Oldsmobile Super "88" Holiday Coupe. A General Motors Value.

NEW, ALL-AROUND-NEW WITH THAT NEW "GO-AHEAD" LOOK!

Flashing into the future with flying colors . . . Oldsmobile for '55! . . . *more spectacular, more colorful, more powerful* than ever! In three exciting series (Ninety-Eight, Super "88", "88"), every one of them new, all-around-new, *all the way through!* All with the commanding new "Go-Ahead" look, all with the terrific response of the new "Rocket" Engine! With bold, sweeping new front-end design . . . dazzling new styling, front to rear! Glorious new interiors, superb new "Rocket" ride—the newest *new ideas on wheels!* And Oldsmobile offers an even wider choice in dramatic new "flying color" patterns. More than ever, Oldsmobile is out ahead to *stay ahead!* See your dealer . . . see these magnificent new, *all-around-new* 1955 "Rocket" Oldsmobiles!

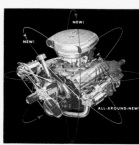

ALL-NEW "ROCKET" 202 ENGINE!
Features new 202 horsepower, higher 8.5-to-1 compression, new power-contoured combustion chambers, high-lift camshaft, new higher torque!

OLDSMOBILE

1955 OLDSMOBILE SUPER "88" HOLIDAY COUPE

Daring . . . dramatic . . . distinctive—it's Oldsmobile's "flying color" styling for 1955! Colors range from soft and quiet to dazzling and brilliant. Treatments go from conservative solids to stunning contrasts! Just think—with more than 100 combinations to choose from, you can almost style your own car! And when you command that new "Rocket" 202 Engine you'll know . . . this is your year to go ahead with Oldsmobile!

The New PACKARD
WITH TORSION-LEVEL RIDE

1955 PACKARD PATRICIANS

More Style, More Power, And a Built-in Future!

1955 PONTIAC 870 CATALINA

Spectacular – from Take-off to Top Performance!

1955 PONTIAC STAR CHIEF
CUSTOM CATALINA

At an All-Time High in Sales and Value!

1955 PONTIAC STAR CHIEF CUSTOM
CATALINA

Most power per dollar in its field!

1955 PONTIAC STAR CHIEF
CONVERTIBLE

1956 BUICK

1956 BUICK ROADMASTER CONVERTIBLE

The Christmas They'll Never Forget!

Cadillac

1956 CADILLAC

YOUR CADILLAC DEALER

Because once you've driven this sweet-handling showboat, the adjectives will take care of themselves. Once you've sampled Chevy's hair-trigger reflexes and nailed-down stability, you'll see why it's one of the few great road cars built today!

Horsepower that ranges up to 225 makes hills flatter and saves precious seconds for safer passing. And the way this Chevrolet wheels around tight turns would gladden the heart of a dyed-in-the-wool sports car fan.

Come in and highway-test this new Chevrolet.

SEE YOUR CHEVROLET DEALER

youth, beauty, Chevrolet, action!

1956 CHEVROLET BEL AIR CONVERTIBLE

What you can learn about cars from firemen!

The '56 Chevrolet

It looks high priced—but it's the new Chevrolet "Two-Ten" 4-Door Sedan

For sooner and safer arrivals!

1956 CHEVROLET TWO-TEN FOUR-DOOR SEDANS

1956 FORD

1956 FORD THUNDERBIRD

8-PASSENGER
COUNTRY SQUIRE
America's most distinguished wagon—combines all-steel body with the traditional beauty of wood-like trim. Like all Ford wagons, it's available with 225-h.p. engine.

8-PASSENGER
COUNTRY SEDAN
The stowaway seat in this 4-door model folds flat into the floor in seconds. With rear seat out and tail gate down, you have nearly nine feet of level load space!

Here's a 4-door beauty that converts from

THE PARKLANE
With wall-to-wall carpeting throughout, here is the most regal of Ford's 2-door, 6-passenger wagons. Converts in seconds. Vinyl cover conceals luggage behind seat.

1956 FORD CONTINENTAL MARK IIS

1956 Oldsmobile "88" Holiday Sedans

1956 Super 88 Holiday Sedan

310 HP CARIBBEAN CONVERTIBLE

The car
with the
POWER
personality!

OLDSMOBILE

You'll be fast friends . . . right from the *start!* All-out action goes with Oldsmobile's inspired new Starfire styling for '56. The Rocket T-350 — mightiest Rocket ever — blazes forth with an emphatic answer to your demand for power. In a flash you streak from standing to cruising . . . ever so smoothly with revolutionary new Jetaway Hydra-Matic*. There's new beauty, new protection, too, with "Intagrille Bumper" design. Stop at our showroom soon!

*Standard on Ninety-Eight models, optional at extra cost on Super 88.

SEE YOUR NEAR
OLDSMOBILE DEA

SAFETY DIFFERENTIAL!

1956 Oldsmobile

1956 Packard "Four Hundred"

They're Driving the Biggest Thrill of the Trip
1956 PONTIAC STRATO-STREAK

1956 Pontiac Catalina

QUEEN
of the Hardtops

Here is a car that received the "custom treatment" all the way. One glance tells you this regal Star Chief Catalina is the most exciting of all the hardtops!

Inside, it surrounds you with soft, hand-buffed top-grain leathers . . . rich nylon . . . lush, deep-pile carpeting. And, on the highway, you'll thrill to the power of its 227-h.p. Strato-Streak V-8 . . . the incomparable

smoothness of its exclusive Strato-Flight Hydra-Matic . . . the brilliant, road-ruling performance of America's most advanced performance team.

Just a few minutes in this lovely and lively creation is royally rewarding. Try it and you'll know—this is the queen of them all!

*An extra-cost option

PONTIAC MOTOR DIVISION OF GENERAL MOTORS CORPORATION

136

ACCELERATION TESTS PROVED PONTIAC'S SIZZLING TAKE-OFF—a standard model Pontiac with the great new 227-h.p.* V-8 engine streaked from 0-60 mph in 10 seconds flat!—45-60 mph in 4 seconds!

They couldn't believe the stop watch!

1956 PONTIAC
STRATO-STREAK

Pontiac

1956 PONTIAC
STRATO-FLIGHT

THE CAR SAYS "GO" AND THE PRICE WON'T STOP YOU—Pontiac's three great lines, with up to 227 horsepower, completely encompass every requirement from peak luxury to low price. You can actually buy a big, glamorous Pontiac 860 for less than 44 models of the low-priced three!
*An extra-cost option.

1956 PONTIAC

860 4-DOOR, 3-seat, with room for 9 passengers . . . both rear seats fold for extra carrying space

FOUR OF AMERICA'S BEST BUYS . . . *for Beauty, Bigness and Blazing Go!*

Why not have fun while you're being practical?
Here are four wonderful ways to do just that! Each one is sleek and exciting as a sports car, handy as a pickup truck . . . and extra *big* in the bargain with a road-leveling 122" wheelbase!

But the really breath-taking difference in Pontiac's fabulous family wagons is the way they GO!

There's nothing like it . . . because they're powered by the greatest performance team ever offered in a station

wagon . . . the mighty 227-horsepower Strato-Streak V-8 and revolutionary Strato-Flight Hydra-Matic Drive*!

That big power means handling ease and liveliness you've never known in a big car before . . . you have to experience it to believe it.

And wait 'til you hear the prices. They're as practical . . . *and exciting* . . . as the cars themselves . . . starting right down with the lowest!

Come in soon and make America's best station wagon buy!
*An extra-cost option.

860 2-DOOR, 2-seat, low-priced suburban favorite available in 48 color combinations

STAR CHIEF SAFARI 2-DOOR, 2-seat custom de luxe style leader

SEE YOUR PONTIAC DEALER

870 4-DOOR, 2-seat, rear seat folds flat for 71½' carrying space with gate closed, 9' gate open

'56 STRATO-STREAK PONTIAC

1956 STUDEBAKERS

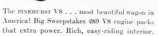

1956 STUDEBAKER

the big news in sports cars...the Studebaker *Hawks*

1957 Buick
Roadmasters

1957 Buick Roadmaster

1957 Buick Century Six-Passenger Two-Door Riviera

1957 Chevrolet Bel Air Sport Coupe

1957 Cadillac

smooth as quicksilver...

and quick as they come...the '57 Chevrolet!

1957 Chevrolet Bel Air Four-Door Sedan

1957 Chevrolet

ANNOUNCING FOR 1957

THE MIGHTY

1957 Chrysler New Yorker

Jewels by Harry Winston

1957 Chevrolet Bel Air Sport Coupe

CHRYSLER

THE MIGHTY CHRYSLER
Most glamorous car in a generation

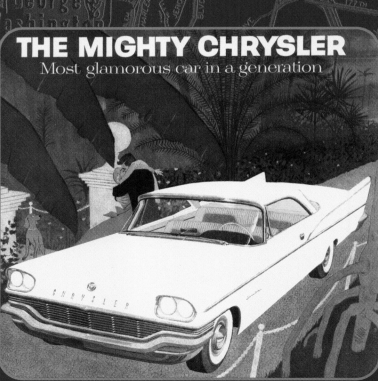

1957 Chrysler Imperial Crown Convertible

1957 Chrysler

Here's your First Class Stateroom in your new kind of FORD!

...and it has that "Touch of Tomorrow," too!

It's like a de luxe suite on 'A' deck!

The new Fairlane 500 Town Victoria ...over 17 feet of long, lean automobile and it stands only 4 feet, 8 inches high.

Luxury cruiser

This is the way to cruise . . . to float over the miles. The New Kind of Ford is a long boat (over 17 feet in the Fairlane Series), a low boat (only 4 feet, 8 inches high), a power boat (with a wide range of horsepowers to meet your every need).*

Those sharp, rakish lines, glittering with the Touch

of Tomorrow, enclose real luxury. From the moment you open heavier precise fitting doors, you are surrounded by a solid, cushiony comfort—as solid as the car itself. For the luxurious comfort goes deep, down into the engineering that rides you with the silent smoothness of a swan on a pond. And you cruise in

*A special 270-hp Thunderbird 312 Super V-8 engine available at extra cost. Also, extra high-performance Thunderbird 312 Super V-8 engine delivering up to 285 hp

color—the rich but delicate new 1957 shades harmoniously keyed throughout, from the heavy, rich-looking looped-rayon carpets to the crush-grain finish on the vinyl seat trim. Every interior detail, from the clean-cut instrument panel to the clean, smooth sweep of the wide-wrap rear window, is styled for fine-car elegance.

And this luxury cruiser sells at the low Ford prices,

despite the fact that it's completely new, from the small wheels that give you a plushier ride to the steering that's so sensitive yet firm that it almost seems to work by thought control. *See the great range of new Fords at your dealer's. Anywhere on land, this is the way to launch yourself in 1957* **at the low Ford price!**

1957 FORD FAIRLANE 500 TOWN VICTORIA

1957 FORD FAIRLANE 500

Wow! Over 17'

The Fairlane 500 Club Victoria: One of 9 Fairlane models in 2 series. All offer luxurious room for 12 knees, 12 elbows and six opera hats.

Picture yourself in the middle of tomorrow...Today!

1957 FORD FAIRLANE 500 CLUB VICTORIA

1. EXCLUSIVE STYLING SHARED BY NO OTHER CAR — Sleek, clean-cut, dynamically different. Notice the distinctive design of the roof. Here's the most advanced car you can buy at any price. Shown above, the Turnpike Cruiser 4-door. Also available in a 2-door model. A 290-hp Turnpike Cruiser V-8 engine is standard in both models.

At the very top of Mercury's dream-car fleet — THE TURNPIKE CRUISER
All the brilliant BIG M features for '57 plus 7 found in no other car!

2-4. NEW BREEZEWAY VENTILATION WITH ROOF-LEVEL AIR INTAKES, NEW SKY-LIGHT DUAL-CURVE WINDSHIELD, NEW RETRACTABLE BACK WINDOW — No other car in America has all of these Turnpike Cruiser features. And you get them at no extra cost. Air is drawn in through the supplementary intakes above the windshield and gently flows out through the power-operated back window. It's the greatest improvement in car ventilation in automotive history. The new windshield wraps up as well as around each side. You can see high traffic lights and mountain scenery without bending . . . the special tinting at the top of the windshield reduces glare.

5-7. NEW MONITOR CONTROL PANEL, TACHOMETER, AVERAGE SPEED COMPUTER The new Monitor Panel is driver-planned for easy seeing and use, and includes such advanced instruments as a Tachometer to check engine rpm's and a new Average-Speed Computer Clock to let you figure your average speed at any point in your trip.

NEW QUADRI-BEAM HEADLAMPS — As functional as they are beautiful. The outside lamps have both high and low beams. The inside units have high beams only. Using all four beams for highway driving produces a far better and brighter pattern of illumination. A foot switch turns off high beams, switches on low.

1957 MERCURY TURNPIKE CRUISER FOUR-DOOR

Bigger all over! Exclusive Floating Ride with Air-Cushion Suspension gives true passenger-car comfort. Here, without question, are the most convenient, luxurious and easiest riding station wagons ever built. Everything is totally new, completely redesigned. New beauty, new spaciousness, new riding comfort — new ideas everywhere you look.

MERCURY ELIMINATES THE LIFT GATE, LOWERS THE TAIL GATE — Nothing to get in the way when you're loading big, bulky objects. And the tail gate is much lower than on many other station wagons — permits much easier loading and unloading.

THERE ARE THREE VIEW-CRAMPING PILLARS IN MOST WAGONS

THERE'S ONLY ONE SIDE PILLAR IN THE NEW MERCURY

THE OPEN-AIR FEELING OF A HARDTOP — Just look — there is a picture-window expanse of glass all around you (more than

1957 MERCURY

THE "HARDTOP" CONCEPT COMES
TO STATION WAGON DESIGN!

NEW 1957 OLDSMOBILE "Fiesta"

1957 OLDSMOBILE FIESTA

1957 OLDSMOBILE
SUPER "88"
HOLIDAY SEDAN

1957 OLDSMOBILE
SUPER 88 FIESTA

1957 OLDSMOBILE
STARFIRE 98
HOLIDAY COUPE

Lucky You!

1957 OLDSMOBILE GOLDEN
ROCKET 88 HOLIDAY COUPE

1957 OLDSMOBILE GOLDEN
ROCKET 88 HOLIDAY COUPE

NEW OBSERVATION SEAT available in 9-passenger Plymouth Sport and Custom Suburbans. More legroom. Folds flush into floor for extra cargo space.

from the Observation Seat of your
BIG, NEW PLYMOUTH SUBURBAN
see how far behind the "other two" are

Here's a dazzling *new kind* of station wagon ...the big Plymouth Suburban! 3 full years ahead! With exciting new features you can't get on any other station wagon in the field!

Just a few of the many important advances are shown on the opposite page. You enjoy them in the biggest...longest...widest ...roomiest station wagon in the low-price 3.

In fact, you can't buy bigger at *any* price! 12 exciting models. 2-door and 4-door. New, higher-power six and terrific new FURY V-8 engines—super-powered up to 290 hp!

(see other page)

1957 PLYMOUTH

1957 PONTIAC

1957 STUDEBAKER

You're face to face with the '58 Buick

1958 Buick

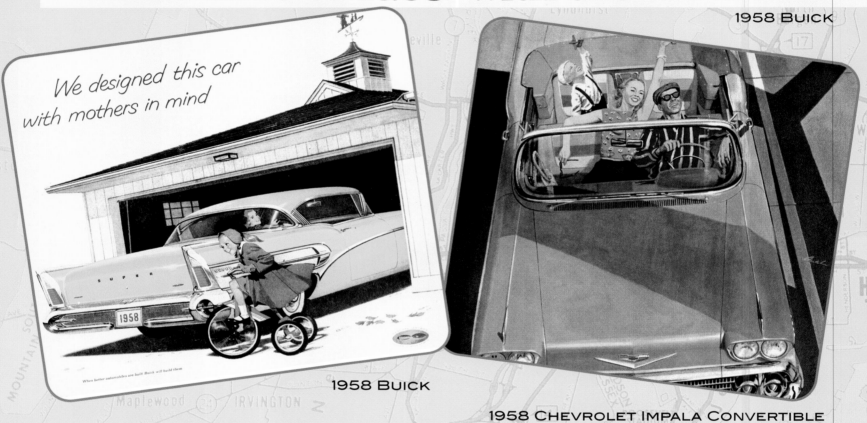

We designed this car with mothers in mind

1958 Buick

1958 Chevrolet Impala Convertible

1958 Chevrolet Bel Air Sport Sedan

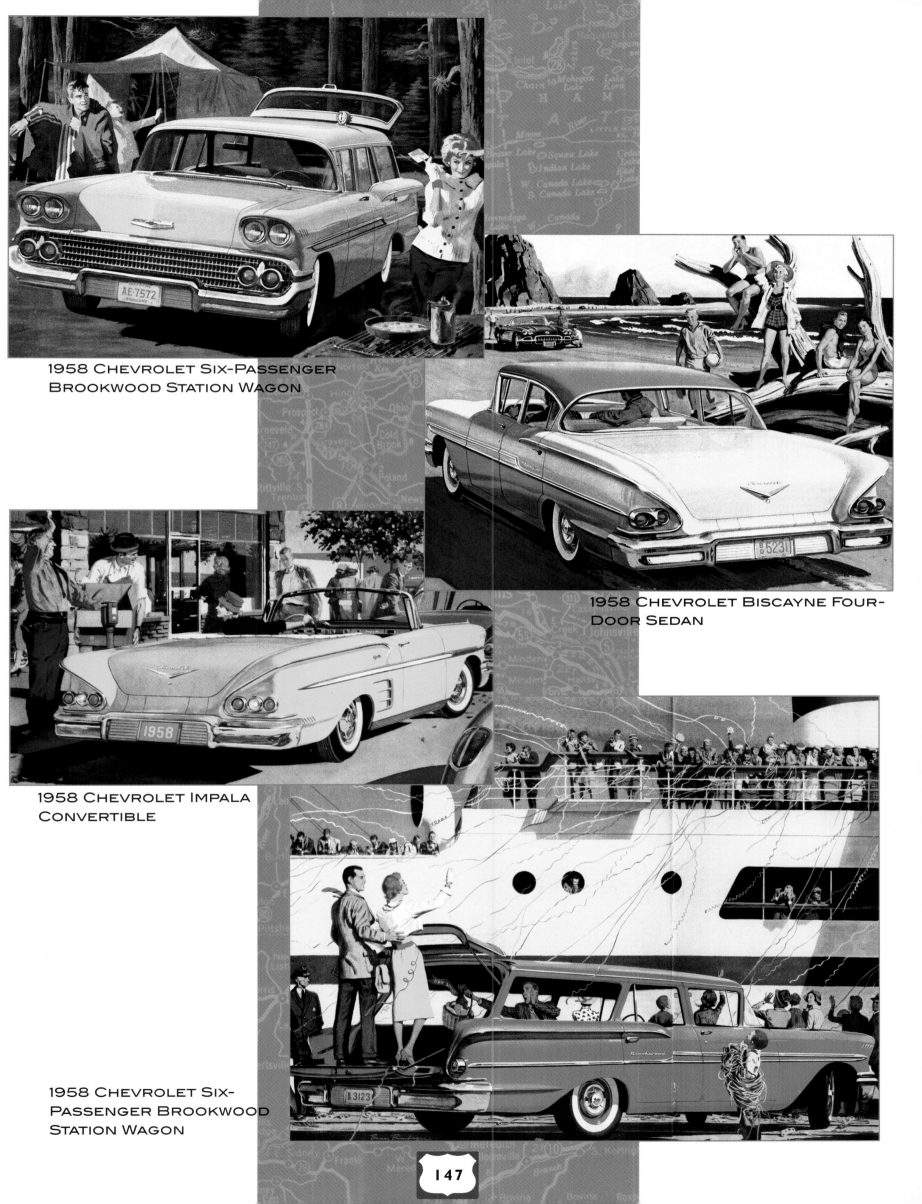

1958 Chevrolet Six-Passenger
Brookwood Station Wagon

1958 Chevrolet Biscayne Four-
Door Sedan

1958 Chevrolet Impala
Convertible

1958 Chevrolet Six-
Passenger Brookwood
Station Wagon

1958 Edsel

**1958 Edsel Citation
Two-Door Hardtop**

1958 Ford Thunderbirds

Portrait of Craftsmanship in Action

The all new *Packard Hawk*

THE MOST ORIGINAL CAR ON THE AMERICAN ROAD

You will find no other car like the Packard Hawk. It is the most original and distinctive automobile crafted in America, styled to match the tempo of our times. Its unique flowing lines are aerodynamic. Its fins: functional. It is designed with that imaginative flair you only expect to find in Europe's most fashionable automobiles. Faithful to its thoroughbred breeding, the Packard Hawk is a *luxury* automobile with smooth, soft leather seats and elegant, tasteful interior appointments.

Extra Power from Built-in Supercharger

Its appearance is complemented by power from a highly efficient V-8 engine with a built-in supercharger, capable of instantaneous acceleration, or smooth

performance under the most trying conditions of stop-and-go traffic. The supercharger with variable speed drive cuts in automatically as needed, for acceleration or extra power for passing or hill climbing, but when not in use, costs nothing extra in gasoline. It is a design for power, with economy.

The Packard Hawk is *the* new car with a regal air that immediately distinguishes its owner as a man of position. Put yourself in that position . . . behind the wheel of a Packard Hawk, soon.

Studebaker-Packard offers the most varied line of cars in America. See them all . . . economy cars . . . sports cars . . . station wagons . . . luxury sedans and hardtops.

Visit your Studebaker-Packard dealer today!

Studebaker-Packard
CORPORATION
Where pride of Workmanship comes first!

1958 PACKARD HAWK

BOLD NEW CHIEFTAIN *Pontiac*

CLEAR-VISION SAFETY PLATE GLASS IN ALL WINDOWS.

Boldest Advance in Low-Price History!

Get an eyeful of Pontiac's Bold New Chieftain, the totally new creation that shatters every low-price-field tradition in size, luxury, handling and response! Here is freshness that literally begins at the foundation of automotive design with a completely new frame, chassis and body. And to make this dream on wheels complete, there are lavish, new color-coordinated interiors, complete with wall-to-wall carpeting, *even in the lowest-priced model!* See and drive this Bold New Chieftain . . . THE LOW-PRICE FIELD NEVER HAD IT SO GOOD!

EVER-LEVEL AIR RIDE—Just one of many bold new features, here's the most perfect suspension system ever developed—and Pontiac's revolutionary Aero-Frame is specifically designed for it! Air cushions on all four wheels literally float you over the bumps . . . keep the car perfectly level even with a 1,000-lb. load!

TEMPEST 395 PERFORMANCE
Try the jeweled-action response of Pontiac's brand-new engine! You can choose from four horsepower ratings—including Tri-Power Carburetion* and Fuel Injection.*
*An extra-cost option.

1958 PONTIAC CHIEFTAINS

BEATS THE BEST OF THE LOW-PRICE 3 . . . FOR LESS MONEY!

CIRCLES-OF-STEEL SAFETY
Pontiac's new body surrounds you with girder-like steel below. Front and rear—and every window of every Pontiac is Safety Plate Glass.

QUADRA-POISE ROADABILITY
Pontiac's revolutionary new frame design and suspension geometry virtually eliminates dive, sway and bounce.

TEMPEST 395 PERFORMANCE
It's exclusively yours in Pontiac—an advanced V-8 power plant built to introduce finer than the finest watches! Try the new jeweled-action response!

EVERYONE LOVES IT—ANYONE CAN AFFORD IT!

If you're considering a so-called "de luxe" model of the low-price three, this Pontiac carries your price tag! Yet not one of the three smaller cars comes even close to Pontiac's genuine big-car size, performance and comfort! And talk about new ideas—in the Golden Jubilee Pontiac you get the boldest advances in 50 years—from the industry's hottest engineering team! And luxury? To discover the lowest-priced Pontiac gives you color-matched interiors and wall-to-wall carpeting! To discover America's Number One Value, visit your Pontiac dealer for a drive and a deal you'll never forget!

PONTIAC MOTOR DIVISION OF GENERAL MOTORS CORPORATION

Bold New Car for a Bold New Generation

BIG BOLD *Chieftain* PONTIAC

THE CAR: BUICK '59

1959 BUICK ELECTRA 225 FOUR-DOOR HARDTOP

THE FLEETWOOD SIXTY SPECIAL

A NEW REALM OF MOTORING MAJESTY

THE 1959 *Cadillac*

By appointment to the world's most discriminating motorists!

THE ELDORADO BIARRITZ

A single glance tells you, beyond any question, *that these are the newest and most magnificent Cadillac cars ever created.* Dazzling in their beauty, enchanting in their grace and elegance, and inspiring in their Fleetwood luxury and decor—they introduce a new realm of motoring majesty. And a single journey at the wheel will reveal still another unquestionable fact—*that these are the finest performing Cadillacs ever produced.* With a spectacular new engine, with a smoother, more responsive Hydra-Matic

drive, and with improved qualities of ride and handling, they provide a totally new sense of mastery over time and distance. This brilliant new Cadillac beauty and this marvelous new Cadillac performance are offered in thirteen individual body styles. To see and to drive any of them is to acknowledge Cadillac a new measure of automotive supremacy. Your dealer invites you to do both at your first opportunity.

CADILLAC MOTOR CAR DIVISION • GENERAL MOTORS CORPORATION

THE SIXTY-TWO COUPE

1959 CADILLAC

Hertz rent it here ...leave it there!

1959 CHEVROLET

EXCITING ESCAPE !
...this lion-hearted call to the open road

TOUCH a fingertip to Chrysler's pushbutton TorqueFlite transmission. Feel how smoothly, how instantly, power surges to your service.

...AND GO for the open road. Give this agile and adventurous car a chance to show you how exciting driving can be!

1959 CHRYSLER

Chrysler Windsor 2-Door Hardtop in Nocturne Blue and Ivory White.

SPACE TRAVEL
...it's pushbutton driving ease with room to spare!

Start your own count-down—at Chrysler's unique control center! **7** Touch button or bar—be with music. **6** Mirror-Matic—flips headlight glare out of your eyes . . . electronically. **5** Your finger—selects warmth, or air-conditioned comfort. **4** Auto-Pilot selector —dial your speed, push the button, forget the gas pedal. **3** Automatic Beam-Changer—politely dims your lights. **2** Control panel for all windows. **1** TorqueFlite pushbuttons —just touch . . . and go! There's space-age magic in each of these wonderful Chrysler options. And for the space-minded traveler: hat-wearing, stretch-out roominess for relaxed adventuring. Enjoy Chrysler's quiet, quality ride, too. It's a lasting tribute to Chrysler's rugged construction. Try it yourself. Drive America's most fully automated car . . .

CHRYSLER DIVISION OF CHRYSLER CORPORATION

lion-hearted **CHRYSLER**
...setting the pace in convenience and comfort

1959 CHRYSLER WINDSOR TWO-DOOR
HARDTOP

Here's how *your* family will find out...
IT PAYS
TO OWN A DODGE

Let's say your family is the kind that wants more than you get in the "low-priced" field. You want more room and comfort. You want more solidness on the road. You want a car that's truly fine in its deep-down quality. And most of all, you want a car you can all enjoy without going "overboard" on purchase price, or on gas and upkeep costs.

So head for your Dodge dealer's—and find a revelation!

The savings start right off the bat! You find that a big, solid Dodge Coronet *costs less to buy* than any car that comes close to it in comfort, roominess, fine-car looks and handling. It pays you $100, $200 or more to choose Dodge over comparable models of other cars in the field. Matter of fact, your Dodge may cost you less than smaller, less substantial models in the low-priced field.

You'll notice the difference in gas bills! In the recent Mobilgas Economy Run, a Dodge V-8 delivered an outstanding 21.74 miles per gallon. Dodge not only finished 1-2 in the low-medium price field, it also topped all other cars from the low-price V-8 field on up. In many other ways—tune-up costs, brake lining wear, spark plug replacement—a Dodge *costs less* to drive.

Your vacation—the "Big Pay-off!" On top of your savings on purchase price, gas economy, upkeep costs—you'll discover how much *more* you get in a Dodge. More room, more comfort. The road-hugging miracle of Torsion-Aire Ride; the security of Total-Contact Brakes and Safety-Rim Wheels all at no extra cost. It's just *more* car for the money!

1959 Dodge

1959 EDSEL

1959 EDSEL CORSAIR FOUR-DOOR
HARDTOP, VILLAGER STATION WAGON

1959 EDSEL

1959 Edsel

59 FORDS are built for people
59 FORDS are built for savings

New Ford Galaxie Club Victoria leaves the others behind with Thunderbird style, Thunderbird "go"!

1959 Ford Galaxie Club Victoria

1959 Ford

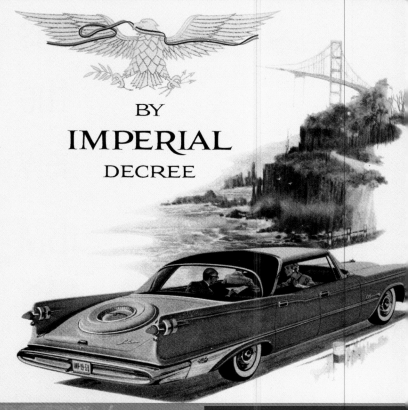

BY
IMPERIAL
DECREE

1959 Imperial

This '59 Oldsmobile wheel in your hands
will introduce you to *That New Olds Feeling.*
A feeling of quality* and refinement...
a feeling of unexcelled comfort and handling ease.
Visit your Oldsmobile Quality Dealer
and drive the smartest looking
Rocket Engine Olds ever built!

QUALITY IS STANDARD EQUIPMENT ON EVERY '59 OLDS!
ABOVE: SUPER 88 HOLIDAY SPORTSEDAN

Proven Quality... standard on every '59 Olds!
Above: Ninety-Eight Convertible Coupe.

1959 Oldsmobiles

1959 Mercury

153

1959 Pontiacs

EXCLUSIVELY YOURS—WIDE-TRACK WHEELS

Wheels moved out a full 5 inches for the widest, steadiest stance in America—better cooling for engine and brakes—lower center of gravity for better grip on the road, safer cornering, smoother ride. *You get the most beautiful roadability in the whole wide world!*

1959 Pontiac

1959 Rambler

1960 Buick Invicta Two-Door Hardtop

1960 Cadillac Coupe de Ville

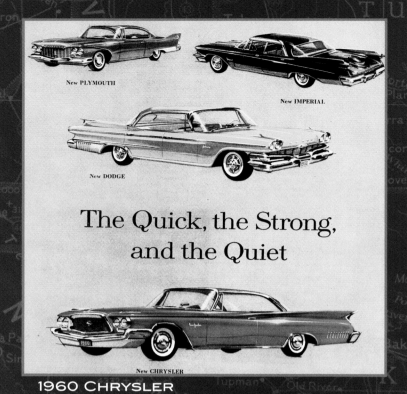

1960 CHRYSLER

1960 CHEVROLET CORVAIR,
IMPALA SPORT SEDAN

1960 CHEVROLET NOMAD STATION WAGON,
CORVAIR MONZA FOUR-DOOR SEDAN

1960 Cadillac Coupe de Ville

1960 Comet

NIFTY!

Enough dash and flair to make sports cars green with envy.

1960 Edsel

1960 Ford Todor Wagon, Fordor
Falcon Wagon

Blessed event for budgets

FORD'S ECONOMY TWINS FOR 1960

Two new Fords...Two new low-price fields...
Two wonderful new ways to go "The Finest"

1960 FORD FALCON,
FAIRLANE 500

1960 LINCOLN CONTINENTAL

1960 LINCOLN FOUR-DOOR LANDAU

1960
OLDSMOBILE
NINETY-EIGHT
HOLIDAY FOUR-
DOOR SPORT
SEDAN

1960 OLDSMOBILE

1960 PONTIAC BONNEVILLE VISTA

1960 OLDSMOBILE

Olds is the car that rockets you out of the ordinary!

When you take the wheel of a '60 Olds, you've found something great . . . and you know it!

You've found new beauty, new grace . . . a rocketing new pace that makes you want to get up and go places! And Olds for '60 is just the car to take you there . . . silently, smoothly and securely.

Make your choice from Oldsmobile's three famous series . . . the Dynamic 88, Super 88 and Ninety-Eight . . . names that mean performance, quality and value to everyone!

Let yourself go for an Oldsmobile . . . at your local authorized Quality Dealer's today!

OLDSMOBILE DIVISION • GENERAL MOTORS CORPORATION

GO OLDS '60!

1960 Pontiac

1960 Pontiac Bonneville Convertible

NEW 1960 RAMBLER CUSTOM CROSS COUNTRY—America's biggest selling compact station wagon now even smarter, thriftier, easier to park. Six or Rebel V-8.

At top right is the brilliant new Rambler Custom Four-Door Sedan for '60.

3 WIDE SEATS, 5 BIG DOORS—Lots of room for the biggest families. The tailgate is a fifth-door with positive outside key lock, so children can't open from inside. Rear passengers step in easily without having to scramble over tailgate or seats. Easier to load, too.

EASY TO ENTER. Rambler's high, wide doors let you *step in*, not *stoop in*. Interior is completely new for 1960—stunning new fabrics, colors. The new instrument panel is beautiful, too, and provides greater safety . . . easy-to-see dials and easy-to-reach controls.

THE WORLD'S LARGEST BUILDER
OF COMPACT CARS ANNOUNCES
The New Standard of Basic Excellence...
NEW RAMBLER FOR '60

1960 Rambler

1961 Buick Special Station Wagon, Le Sabre Four-Door Hardtop

1961 Cadillac Sedan de Ville

Corvair 95 Rampside—with a wing-ding of an idea for easy loading! Ramp is nearly 4 feet wide.

1961 Chevrolet Corvair

THE ONLY COMPACT
WITH FINE-CAR STYLE,
BIG-CAR RIDE
AND FAMILY SIZE . . .

Comet
THE BETTER COMPACT CAR

1961 Comet

This Corvair 700 4-Door Sedan has heating ducts built right into its Body by Fisher.

More happy ideas from the new

more spunk, savings and travel space!

'61 CHEVY CORVAIR!

Wasn't easy, but we managed to make Corvair even more desirable in '61: we boosted the displacement of that air-cooled rear engine to 145 cubic inches for spunkier performance. Made Corvair even thriftier to run: you get more miles per gallon plus quicker cold-start warmup to get you saving sooner. (There's a new heater* that warms everyone evenly, and a longer range fuel tank.) Added space inside for you, up front for your luggage. (Sedans and Coupes give you nearly 12% more space under the hood.) You'll like Corvair's smoother, smarter styling, too, the minute you lay eyes on it. But that's not the half of Corvair's good news for '61. Now Corvair has family-lovin' wagons for you!

*optional at extra cost

The Lakewood 700 Station Wagon—4 doors and up to 68 cubic feet of cargo area.

The Lakewood Station Wagon does a man-sized job with cargo, yet handles like a charm. Our Greenbrier Sports Wagon—unlike anything ever built in America before—has space for up to 175.5 cubic feet of people and things on a maneuverable 95" wheelbase. Check *that* against the wagons you're used to. Same rear-engine traction, same parkability that have become a Corvair trademark. See the whole sensible lineup soon—at your Chevrolet dealer's.

1961 Chevrolet Corvair

beautifully proportioned to the CLASSIC FORD LOOK

Here is the eternally beautiful Galaxie Club Victoria in Rome's famous Piazza del Campidoglio

BEAUTIFULLY BUILT TO TAKE CARE OF ITSELF

1961 Ford Galaxie Club Victoria

FALCON '61 has these wonderful birthday presents for you!

1961 Ford Falcon

1961 Lincoln Continental

1961 Mercury Monterey

The beauty about a Mercury...

It's all this: exciting styling, famous Mercury room, economy, pep. And most beautiful of all...every Mercury is now in the popular-price range.

1961 Oldsmobile

Tantalizing Beauty...
Skyrocket "Go"!
'61 OLDS

1961 Oldsmobile
Ninety-Eight

1961 Oldsmobile F-85

1961 PONTIAC BONNEVILLE

1961 PONIAC BONNEVILLE SPORTS COUPE

1962 CADILLAC COUPE DE VILLE

1962 CHEVROLET IMPALA FOUR-DOOR SPORT SEDAN

1962 Corvette Shark

Look at its big-car features —and you'll think the low price is a misprint!

The Ford Fairlane idea is this: give people the fine features they look for in big cars— and put a compact price tag on them. Give people big-car room, ride, quality and performance—and then surprise them with compact-car handling and economy. Have your cake and eat it, too? The 1962 Ford Fairlane says yes—in a way no other car can.

This is what Fairlane gives you that the compacts don't

Big-car room. Big as some of the roomiest cars in Ford history.

Big-car ride. A full 115½" wheelbase.

Big-car performance. All-new Challenger V-8 engine (optional).

Twice-a-year service. 6,000 miles between routine service stops.

Fine-car luxury. Upholsteries and appointments equalled only in cars costing hundreds more.

This is what Fairlane gives you that the big cars don't

Low price. Hundreds less than previous Fairlanes . . . well under many compacts.

Economy. World's first Economy V-8 (optional). Or, for even greater savings, the new Fairlane Six.

Painless parking. A full foot shorter than other full-size cars . . . fits easily in tight spots.

Handy handling. It's compact-trim, compact-nimble.

Great garaging. 197" length makes garages big again.

FORD *Fairlane*

FORD *Fairlane* 500
RIGHT BETWEEN GALAXIE AND FALCON

1962 Ford Fairlane and Fairlane 500

PRESENTING... *Ninety-Eight*
OLDSMOBILE *for* '62

1962 OLDSMOBILE NINETY-EIGHT
HOLIDAY SPORTS SEDAN

A PICNIC TO DRIVE...*a pleasure to own!*

Ask any member of the outdoor crowd...he'll tell you: Oldsmobile's F-85 is the perfect pick for *any* picnic. It's engineered to roam the raggedest country lanes with nimble smoothness! Sized to seat six with ease (lunch baskets and all)! And powered by an aluminum V-8 engine that takes any hill with never a second breath! Try it! Fun-drive an F-85 today!

OLDS F-85

OLDSMOBILE DIVISION • GENERAL MOTORS CORPORATION

1962 OLDSMOBILE F-85

DARING DESIGN...
RARING TO GO!

1962 OLDSMOBILE

1962 PONTIAC

1962 PONTIAC GRAND PRIX

1962 PONTIAC BONNEVILLE

1963 BUICK LeSABRE

STUDEBAKER
invites your inspection
of a distinctive new family sports classic
The Gran Turismo
Hawk
designed and made in the meticulous tradition of
the great European road cars and offering
the comforts and conveniences
preferred by the discerning
American motorist

• The embodiment of roadability and driving ease from the gleaming expanse of hood through the smallest hand-crafted detail.

• Full 120" wheelbase; Thunderbolt V-8 OHV engine; 3 speed synchromesh transmission standard. Optional floor-mounted 4-speed gear box or Automatic.

• Variable-rate front coil springs and anti-sway bar; asymmetrical rear springing; telescopic shock absorbers; finned-drum brakes.

• True Gran Turismo interiors: full five-passenger capacity; sports car type bucket seats forward, let-down arm rest in rear, optional reclining seats.

• Luxury-padded safety dash, recessed instrumentation. Rich, pleated vinyl upholstery, deep pile carpet. Exquisite detail in all appointments.

• The long list of Gran Turismo Hawk options include: Hill-Holder, limited slip differential, air conditioning.

1962 STUDEBAKER GRAN TURISMO HAWK

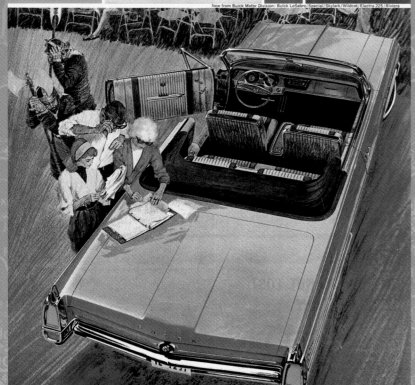

1963 BUICK LESABRE

1963 CHEVROLET CORVETTE

1963 CHEVROLET IMPALA SPORT COUPE

1963 CHRYSLER

1963 OLDSMOBILES

AN OLDSMOBILE ORIGINAL... AMERICA'S FULL-SIZE SPORTS CAR SENSATION!

ANNOUNCING FOR 1963...

Starfire

1963 OLDSMOBILE STARFIRE

Pure glamor...with a touch of adventure

Meet America's full-size sports car sensation—Starfire by Oldsmobile! This spirited pace-setter has *everything!* Styl that's highlighted by a uniquely contoured rear window. Th famous ultra high-compression Starfire V-8 Engine. Sport; leather-trimmed bucket seats. A fashionable front-to-bac control console with stick-shift Hydra-Matic, glove box an tachometer. There's even a brand-new Tilt-Away Steerin Wheel* that adjusts seven ways for ease of entry, exit an driving comfort. Like your action tailored in glamor? Jus drive a '63 Starfire—coupe or convertible—today! Oldsmobil

1963 PONTIAC BONNEVILLE

1963 PONTIAC

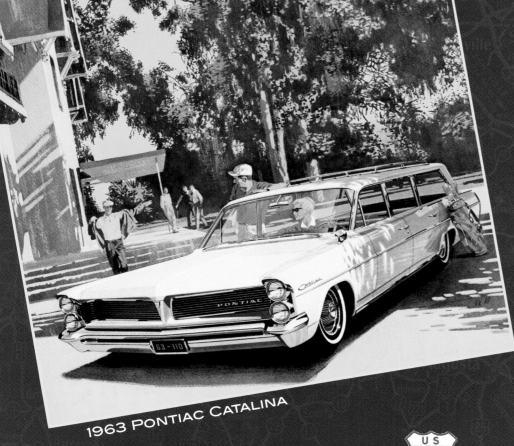

1963 PONTIAC CATALINA

1963 STUDEBAKER
AVANTI

1964 CHEVROLET
MONZA SPYDER
CONVERTIBLE

About the only thing that can come between
a Corvair owner and his Corvair is

1964 CHEVROLET
CORVAIR MONZA
CLUB COUPE

1964 CHRYSLER

MOVE UP TO CHRYSLER '64
1964 Chrysler

Meet the new '64
OLDS F-85 →
...where the action is!

1964 Oldsmobile F-85

1964 Oldsmobile F-85 Cutlass

1964 Oldsmobile F-85

1964 PONTIAC BONNEVILLE

1964 PONTIAC BONNEVILLE

1964 PONTIAC BONNEVILLE

1964 PONTIAC BONNEVILLE

1965 MERCURY
COMET

1965 MERCURY COMET

1965 MERCURY

1965 PONTIAC

1965 PONTIAC BONNEVILLE

1965 PONTIAC BONNEVILLE

Pontiac Grand Prix
If you had two wishes, what would the second one be?

1965 PONTIAC GRAND PRIS

1965 Buick Skylark